# PARENTING ON PURPOSE

Stan E. DeKoven, Ph.D.

Parenting On Purpose

Copyright applied for 1996 by Dr. Stan DeKoven
ISBN: 1-884213-69-3

All rights in this study guide are reserved world-wide
No part of the book may be reproduced in any manner whatsoever without the written permission of Vision Publishing, except for brief quotations embodied in critical articles or reviews.

For information on reordering please contact:

**Vision Publishing
1520 Main Street, Suite C
Ramona, CA 92065
(760) 789-4700**

www.vision.edu

**All scripture references are taken from the New American Standard version of the Bible unless otherwise noted, used by permission.**

**Printed in the United States of America**

# Table of Contents

Forward ................................................................................................5

Introduction .........................................................................................7

Chapter 1
    Parenting: What a Concept ........................................................17

Chapter 2
    Where it Began ..........................................................................23

Chapter 3
    A Look Back ..............................................................................33

Chapter 4
    The Word on Parenting ..............................................................49

Chapter 5
    The Word on Discipline .............................................................61

Chapter 6
    Discipline on Purpose ................................................................69

Chapter 7
    Development: Key to the Child's Kingdom ................................89

Chapter 8
    Environmental Impact ................................................................97

Chapter 9
    Understanding Children's Goals ...............................................109

Chapter 10
    Consequences ..........................................................................123

Appendices .......................................................................................127

Bibliography ....................................................................................139

# Forward

Parenting in the Western world has become an intensely complex responsibility. Even 50 years ago, the roles and responsibilities for men and women were quite simple. Fathers worked, went to war, and protected their families. Their home was their castle. Their children were to fear and adore them. Moms were to cook, clean, have children and remain focused on the family alone. Oh how things have changed.

In our swirling caulstrom called Western civilization, most all of life has been turned up side down. Women, in many ways justifiably so, are demanding the rights of labor outside of the home, sharing of domestic chores, while expecting the man of the house to continue to bring home the "bacon." Men are rarely honored. Many are seen as the present cause of all society ills. Yet, have their roles of authority and importance been challenged and changed? Seldom are parents prepared in the slightest way to assume the awesome role of guide for their unsuspecting children. Limited training is given. Advice is widespread but contradictory, advocating both liberal ideas and a return to "the good old days" which, from what I hear, were not really that good!

Though many volumes have been written on this most important of topic, few attempt to present with clarity the combined full counsel of God, married with practical wisdom and common sense.

For the reader of this or any book, it is vital to seek the highest authority to speak authoritatively on a given subject. The highest authority is a revelatory understanding of the Biblical record, combined with the vast wealth of information available from the study of human behavior over many years. It is further vital that any work be written so that the general reader can read it. It is the hope of the author that this work will be a positive addition to parents understanding of their important role and add ammunition to slay the dragon of this difficult but possible and even joyous task.

# Introduction

It was with great delight that I read an article found in the Ladies Home Journal, dated July 1996. The title of the article is **"Why Are Today's Parents Such Wimps?"** by Leslie Bennett. What a profound question. The article, written with keen insight and humor, presents only too true scenarios of frustrated parents and out of control children. Her premise is that all too often, children are running the home, rather than parents taking their proper place of prominence. She offers several reasons for this national phenomenon and some insightful solutions. They are worth noting.

First, parents today are under unique pressures. Parents are torn apart by the various demands of family and work responsibilities, and are often filled with guilt. Finding the time for childrearing is ever more challenging. The parents, because of the guilt they feel, are often unwilling to discipline their children for fear the children will resent or even hate them. They will therefore placate the child for the sake of peace and quite. Further, many baby boomers, raised in the "Me" generation, have learned permissiveness and passivity, as a response to the rebellion against previous generations. Unfortunately, this passivity and permissiveness has created insecurity in parents, to the place where action is absent when required for the proper care of children. In rejecting the parenting models of previous generations (some of which was **not** healthy, and deserved rejection!) where parents were authoritarian and ruled as benevolent (hopefully) dictators, parents of today have limited experience in parenting with effectiveness, seemingly lost as to what to do when Johnny says "NO!" Adding insult to injury, parents are depicted in the media as the brunt of adolescent jokes, having no clue as to what their children are doing or how to manage their impulsive and self absorbed behavior. Setting limits on children's' behavior has become a lost art form. To set limits is one of the most important of parenting tasks.

The author suggests (based upon *Love & Limits* by Crary) five major limits for healthy child rearing. They are: avoid problems when possible, by controlling the environment in advance of a potential problem, rewarding cooperation, acknowledging feelings, setting limits, and teaching new skills. Further, Gosman *Spoiled Rotten: Today's Children and How to Change Them* (Villard, 1992) provides different insights, including communicate love, follow through with reasonable consequences, model self-esteem, devote lots of time to the child, and remember that the child who has everything appreciates nothing. Very good advice for today's forlorned parents.

Indeed, parenting in the modern world of today is an increasingly difficult task. Even within the church parents experience difficulty in knowing what is right to do in disciplining a child, and who to listen to for advice. The proliferation of experts on what should be a fairly delightful process (parenting) has not provided greater clarity, but has helped to muddy the waters.

## A Biblical Perspective

Before beginning to study so vital a subject as parenting, it is important to review the writer's perspective and purpose. Everyone has a bias that must be taken into account to fully understand his or her viewpoint. It is my hope that many will share or at least withhold judgment on my perspective until a thorough reading of this book is completed.

Let me state categorically that my hermeneutical perspective is conservative, evangelical and charismatic. That is, I am a firm believer in the inspiration of the revealed truth (the Bible) of God's Word, in the relevance of the scripture for daily practice. However, I must give some caution to the above statement. Flexibility must be shown in regards to a specific and often rigid interpretation of a single passage of scripture. Without reference to cultural context, level of psychological or sociological understanding and especially taking into account the worldview of the writer at the time the scripture was written; error in interpretation of scripture is inevitable. I am a strong proponent of a literal translation of scripture whenever possible, yet at times we must understand that a literal interpretation may violate a higher biblical principle such as in the story of the Prodigal and his father. In this story the principle of love, redemption and restoration supersede the law of justice, punishment and retribution. Let me provide another example taken from the book of Deuteronomy chapter 6:1-9,

> *"These are the commands, decrees and laws the Lord your God directed me to teach you to observe in the land that you are crossing the Jordan to possess, so that you, your children and their children after them may fear the Lord your God as long as you live by keeping all his decrees and commands that I give you, and so*

*that you may enjoy long life. Hear, O Israel, and be careful to obey so that it may go well with you and that you may increase greatly in a land flowing with milk and honey, just as the Lord, the God of your fathers, promised you. Hear, O Israel: The Lord our God, the Lord is one. Love the Lord your God with all your heart and with all your soul and with all your strength. These commandments that I give you today are to be upon your hearts. Impress them on your children. Talk about them when you sit at home and when you walk along the road, when you lie down and when you get up. Tie them as symbols on your hands and bind them on your foreheads. Write them on the doorframes of your houses and on your gates."* (NIV)[1]

Obviously, the primary scriptural principle expressed by the author is that of the importance of obeying God's Word, incorporating it into ones life, so that the heart might be transformed to love God and our fellowman. The procedure given by Moses and still embraced by Orthodox Jewry today, for the incorporation of God's Word in lives and to provide a continual reminder, was to place it literally on the forehead in a small container. Bind up your hand with a cord like putting a thread on your finger as a reminder and placing the laws of God in a small container on the doorpost of one's house.

Many in Solomon's day and today have the letter of the law, a Bible on the coffee table, a cross on the wall, etc., yet rarely darken the doors of the church nor allow God's word to penetrate their hearts and modify their lifestyle. If one takes too literally various scriptural edicts, out of proper context, they can actually lead to ungodly and unbiblical responses. Thus, as you read this book it is vitally important to keep an open mind and heart and allow the concepts presented to impact your life. Where the Holy Spirit speaks, be willing to change.

## Problematic Possibilities

Parenting, what a concept! It still amazes me that just 20 years ago our first child was miraculously brought into the world. It seems like just yesterday. Unlike most parents, who have little or no knowledge of positive parenting, my wife Karen and I had studied extensively on the

---

[1] For an expanded perspective on this topic, see Solomon's treatment from Prov. 3:21-22 and 6:21, found in Dr. Chant's *Pentecostal Pulpit* Chapter 12.

topic. Of course, neither book learning nor practical experience such as day care, baby-sitting, etc. can truly prepare someone for the impact and change that an ever so small yet precious child can bring into their life.

However versed you may be in the act and service of care giving more can be learned.

This book attempts to succinctly yet fully provide to the reader a clear understanding of how to purposely, with goal and direction, raise children in this most complex world. The combined wisdom of over twenty years of counseling troubled families, mixed with biblical wisdom are shared with a dash of humor and a spot of realism. Remember, if perfect parenting was a requirement for anything, even God would fail the test. Adam and Eve are just the beginning.

The focus that is presented here is based upon a basic premise, which is very important for the reader to consider. It is based upon a very unique theory, I think. That is, "If I would have never had parents, I would have never had a problem." Most of you will grasp that momentarily, because this is a reality in our lives. If we would have never had parents, we would never have had a problem. There is only one small glitch with my theory, "If we never had parents, we would not be here!"

There is no such thing as a perfect parent. There are all different kinds, in all different shapes, sizes and colors with different temperaments, different styles of discipline, teaching and training. They run in style from hands on constantly, to totally hands off. Many have had parents who have been wonderful blessings and others have had parents that the very thought of brings anxiety into their lives.

In this volume we are going to look at several important concepts. First, what is parenting really all about. Secondly, the purpose that God has for everyone called to the role of parent. We will also explore the similarities that can be found in children, and a number of different concepts with practical application of those concepts for our individual lives as parents.

## Murphy's Law of Parenthood: A Perspective

In truth, what many parents' experience is called <u>Murphy's Law of Parenthood</u>. It will be helpful to look at these things, because they will provide a humorous perspective on what we are going to be discussing in this book.

#1  If your baby sleeps for eight consecutive hours, none of those hours will fall between 11 PM and 7 AM. How many parents have suffered this, especially with brand new babies?

#2  The number of times your child will ask *why* is directly proportional to the length of the book you are reading them. If it is one of those children's books with only a word or two per page, they won't say anything, but if you are in a hurry and they ask for a Dr. Seuss' book, not a page will go by without them asking, "Why are those eggs green?" Children are quite curious of course. Have you ever noticed?

#3  The day your new carpeting is installed, your child will introduce you to projectile vomiting. Unless, of course, it is stain master carpet in which case the child will manage to hit either the sofa or the recliner, whichever one has not been treated with scotch guard. Children have wonderful ways of expressing themselves!

#4  When you finally have your new pastor over for dinner, your child will utter their first word. The good news is that their enunciation is perfect, the bad news is the word that leaves their lips is the worst word you can imagine.

I love Sunday School. Children say the strangest things about mom and dad, especially about things they did last night. "You know what they said about pastor!" You ought to sneak in there sometimes and hear what the children have to say.

#5  Just when you have convinced your pastor that your child did not know what he was saying, the child will utter the second word of their life. The good news is, it is not the same as the first word. The bad news is you realized that their first word was not really the worst one you could have imagined.

#6  When you dress your child in underwear instead of a diaper, they will refuse to tell you when they have to go potty. The only exception is when you are in a baseball stadium filled with fifty-five thousand screaming fans. It is the bottom of the ninth with the bases loaded and your team is down by three that is when your child will utter the words you have been waiting a month to hear. "Daddy, I have to go potty."

#7 Earlier that day you read a magazine article suggesting that if you ignore them now, they will get some kind of complex and become a chronic bed wetter until their college graduation. Or, worse perhaps, your favorite player keeps fouling off three and two pitches until you arrive at the men's room at which point the batter belts a history making grand slam. There is no justice in this world!

#8 The first time your child makes you proud by answering the phone all by themselves, you will find out they hung up on Ed McMahan.

#9 If you are watching your weight, your child will not touch the food they insisted on ordering at a restaurant and you will feel obligated not to let it go to waste.

#10 If you go out to eat and intentionally order light anticipating the opportunity to clean your child's plate, they will finish every last bite.

(Source unknown, my apologies and thanks).

Children are wonderfully and incredibly unpredictable. They are marvelous. They are called in the Bible, "gifts from God." They are a gift that keeps on taking. I've heard prospective parents say, "Well, we're going to wait a few years until we can afford children." You can never afford them. Nor can you make more money than they have the ability to spend.

It is amazing what children can do to alter your lifestyle. Most people, when they get married, start out with absolute wedded bliss. They are happy. Remember those days of being happy. Some of you still remember those days; when you were...happy. You know, that was before the children arrived. Now, of course you had this wonderful child come into your house because you wanted to express your love. Ha, ha, ha, ha. Somebody sang a song, "What's love got to do with it?" Later you will look back and say, "Why? We had a good world. Why did we want to mess it up with children?"

Children do change our lives. They change our lives dramatically because of the very nature that children have, which is one of total dependence upon us to care for them. Most of us know, from a serious viewpoint, that it is a great privilege to have children and a privilege to raise them. It is a wonderful thing to see your children succeed, grow and hopefully become better than what you ever dreamed you could become. Most parents I talk with have great dreams and hopes for their children. Unfortunately, children have their own agenda, and at times can stray in unpleasant even dangerous directions. *Parenting On Purpose* will lay a foundation that can provide for better and more informed choices. However, ultimately, children will eventually exercise their God given right to choose. Now a look at the foundations.

*"Now the man had relations with his wife eve, and she conceived and gave birth to Cain, and she said, 'I have gotten a manchild with the help of the Lord"*

**Genesis 4:1**

# Chapter 1

## Where It Began

One of the most frequently asked questions by concerned parents is "how can we keep our children from going their own direction, from choosing a wrong or unhealthy path"? Well there are no guarantees. However, there are steps a parent can take to minimize their risk and maximize their effectiveness in this very difficult task. But a preliminary question must be asked before the previous one. How does one become a parent (not in the biological sense, which is fairly well known), and how can I know I am ready for the job?

Parenting, what a concept! How do we learn to parent? How many men and women have taken a high school class on "How to Parent?" Even if such a course was offered and was taken, which is doubtful, one would probably remember very little practical from the content. However, all people *do* have a concept of parenting, remembered and acted upon. It was not learned from a class or a book, but all of God's creation has a parenting style, inherited or modeled after those who have gone before. All humans over the age of 10 are junior psychologists. That is, there is a common belief that the reasons for others behaviors are knowable and easily determined. It takes very little research to validate this statement. If you do not think so, just ask anybody. Why did so and so do such and such? They will have a theory. Everyone has an idea of another's motivation or behavior. Unfortunately, they are rarely correct, but at least they have an opinion that they will religiously hold to.

Most everyone believes himself or herself to be an expert on parenting. This is especially true of the parents of the children that they are trying to parent. They know exactly what their child needs all the time, because *they are the parents*. They automatically act according to learned patterns, believed to be right, proper, even perfect! Most do not take the time to think about their thinking, that is, explore how ideas, belief systems, and attitudes about the topic of parenting are developed. The tendency is for parents to function on automatic pilot, assuming that, since I am an adult, and I have had a child, I can be a parent. After all, my spouse and I (at least we hope they are married), were able to produce a baby, so we must know how to be parents." What an absurd but common belief. Simply because one can operate a vehicle does not assume knowledge on its' proper repair and maintenance.

Well then, how does one learn to parent? Some would blame negative parenting on various childhood or family problems in society, especially such morally questionable activities such as television or the secularized Western educational system. Certainly these activities carry some of the responsibility, but are not likely to go away in our lifetime. Some would lay primary blame the church, since the church does not normally teach on subjects such as parenting. In fact, the church has only recently begun to emphasize the importance of teaching on family life. Some topics remain somewhat taboo. An example is the subject of sex. Most churches do teach about sex. They just say, "Do not!" until one gets married, then they say, "Do!" Unfortunately, that is the extent of many a church's sex education teaching. Do not, then do. Without question, the church needs to teach more openly and frequently on these and many other vital subjects, to include that of parenting. However, with the overwhelming responsibility of pastoral care and ministry in general, it seems less than fair to place overly critical blame at the feet of the church and its servants.

Men and women often assume that the ability to parent is learned instinctively, in a similar way as in the animal kingdom. Please understand that humans are not dogs! Mankind does not carry the same level of instinct that the animal kingdom does. A vast majority of behavior is learned, though the learning process is not always easy to understand. Most people learn how to do things in a style that is functional for themselves, and within the society they were raised in. People will frequently attempt to bring blame for parenting problems. Yet, most parents have learned from a number of sources the relative skills of how to parent, whether functionally or dysfunctionally.

The primary source for learning family life and parenting skills is from one's own family of origin. What a frightening thought! "You mean, I learned to be a parent from my mother or father?" Yes. Perhaps from a grandmother or older siblings as well. In some cases, other strong influences in life have demonstrated models for interaction, communication, and for discipline. Whether one likes it or not, the primary source for learning a personal parenting style comes from years of teaching in the school of mom and dad.

I can still remember the first time I uttered these words, "this is going to hurt me more than it is going to hurt you," as I was getting ready to spank one of my children. I could not believe my own ears. How could I have said such a stupid thing, especially since I had previously sworn I would *never* say such a thing to *my* kids!

The first time a parent says or does something that creates a flash of distant memory, it can resound as a profound shock. If one is wise, this day will be the day in which repentance in sackcloth and ashes begins! At least most parents will want to repent, since they most likely feel as though the sins of the fathers have truly and completely invaded their minds. Many, if not most parents have sworn or made a vow, stating something to the effect that, "I am not going to be the kind of parent my parents were." How many of us have ever made that inner vow to be different, perhaps more sober or kind to our children? This vow is so very common. Parents try to keep the vow with due diligence, but often fail in the heat of Junior's trail of tears.

The problem is that all parents have had eighteen plus years of daily contact with their own parents who have modeled a comprehensive parenting style of discipline, correction, communication, etc. that becomes incorporated into the perception of the world. Most often, the eyes that adults look through, when looking their or other children, are a combination of the parents eyes and at least two to eight sets of eyes behind them, going back generationally to grandparents and even great grandparents. All parents, without intervention of additional knowledge will look at their children through the perspective of their family background or family tree.

It is most rare to find someone willing to take the time to explore their own family tree, to review the good and the bad of the parenting that they received. Instead, the tendency is to unconsciously repeat the parenting patterns of previous generations as though in an amnesiac fog. Some so thoroughly and clearly repeat the patterns that they have learned, assuming that what they are doing is morally and psychologically right, healthy, even God ordained; because, if it was good enough for mom and dad, it is good enough for me.

On the other hand, unfortunately, some will explore their family dynamics and will in disdain reject fully their family style. They will vow to do the exact opposite of their parents. When this vow is made, there comes with it a tendency to correct too far to the other side. Still, it is important to remember the majority of people operate as parents on automatic pilot. They are conducting one's parenting based upon what has been unconsciously learned or rejected, without thought as to God's purpose for an individual child. Parenting needs to be based upon the good of the child and the properly understood word of God. May God help to open the eyes of Christian parents to begin to see His plan and purpose for effective parenting.

*"For this cause a man shall leave his father and his mother, and shall cleave to his wife; and they shall become one flesh."*

**Genesis 2:24**

# Chapter 2

# A Look Back

It is vitally important, in light of ones past parental models, to explore effectively and efficiently a personal parental history. As mentioned before, few people will take the time to ask themselves the difficult questions regarding learned behaviors and attitudes. The truth is that most do not consider the need for such self-exploration. Since the bible states that one is to deny self, and take up the cross, what good does self-exploration accomplish? The fact is that in order to take up ones cross (or ones purpose) it is necessary to understand where one has come from. History is the best predictor of present and future behavior. Each child is somewhat different from every other, requiring a unique approach to assist it in reaching its potential in God. Parents may assume that since one is smarter, stronger, and seemingly more capable, and since they have survived their own childhood, having traveled this road before, they must therefore be effective in parenting. Nothing could be further from the truth. Through many years of counseling families, it isn't necessarily so.

Good people who love God with all of their heart - spirit filled people - mess up tremendously in terms of parenting. Not because they do not love God, or do not love their children, but that they are **brain damaged**! Of course, this is not to say that parents are literally organically impaired, but that they have been so brain washed by society, so brain washed by friends, so brain washed by their own family of origin, that they cannot parent on purpose. They do not focus on doing what is required to be able to raise their children in a manner pleasing to God.

To complicate parenting even more, we must realize that there is a natural blending of at least two sets of eyes in each parent, looking at the child in question. Behind the individual mom or dad are the eyes and opinions of the family of origin, inherited from their families. Not only is there the husband's view of what parenting and family is all about, but one must consider (regardless of how chauvinistic the man may be) the wife's opinion, which generally comes from an entirely different viewpoint. Even if a couple is culturally the same, they are still going to have parenting styles that will be extremely different, based upon the divergent family backgrounds.

There are more complications. Many people today come from broken homes. Their model of child raising is based upon an inaccurate or fragmented model. Either the mother or the father has raised them. This often means that they did not have the other parent's primary influence. They may not know what it is like to be a parent or even a spouse. For these, what is the responsibility or the role of a husband, of a wife, according to God's standards? How is the average Christian adult to effectively parent when they have so many conflicting voices in their heads?

Of course, every believer knows the necessity of a thorough reading of the word of God. Most Christians have heard sermons on or have read many passages on marriage and family, becoming familiar with the concepts. Though one may understand the concepts on marriage and family, it is much more difficult to act on them, making them a part of a personal lifestyle. Because of years and years and years of data that says, "Do it this way!" most believers have significant trouble applying biblical truth. Thus, it is essential for every believer to begin to understand themselves, both from the natural or from what has been learned (from faulty parents, friends, media, even church) and the spiritual, from God's Word and Godly counsel.

## An Example

My parents are wonderful and a bit crazy! Yes, that would be the word. They know they are, so it is not a new revelation to them. My mom was an only child; my dad was an only child. They had both been abused as children in one way or another. Both had experienced the devastation of rejection and abandonment, which is the natural result of divorce and remarriage and divorce again. They had limited stability in terms of role models. They each had a mother who figured prominently in their lives and upbringing, but neither one had a father figure, which provided a positive model worth emulating. How did that affect my mom? She had no idea what male - female relationships were like. How did it effect my dad? He had no concept of masculinity issues. Both had to figure out on their own what a husband/father, wife/mother was to be like.

When they found each other, it was quite romantic. They met in a skating rink in San Diego. They relate that the lights just dimmed, except for the light on each other as they skated around the rink. They saw each other and it was passion at first sight. Six weeks later they were married. This was somewhat the norm just after World War II. Couples got married because they did not know if the world was going to blow up, and most got married to have children. Nowadays, couples who bother to get married at all do so for personal enjoyment, pleasure, self-fulfillment and other self oriented objectives. Eventually they might have children when they can either afford them or become so bored with each other that they require a significant and nearly permanent diversion in their lives. An eighteen to twenty-five yearlong diversion!

So my parents came together. What was my father looking for? He was looking for a wife, a mother, a support, a confidant, and a friend. His need was for someone who would encourage him, taking care of all his emotional wounds from the past. What was my mother looking for? She was looking for a man, a strong man who was sensitive, warm and loving. One who would do the dishes, pick up after himself and take care of her. One who would treat her the way she imagined a true prince charming would treat a "princess." Of course, my wonderful father tried but miserably failed because he did not have enough skill or grace to be the perfect husband, and my wonderful Mother failed equally because she did not have the necessary tools to be the perfect wife. Of course, no one is perfect, and thanks to the grace and mercy of the Lord they have become most of the things they dreamed about in the beginning. Thank the Lord for His long-suffering love, and for His work of salvation in us all.

When my parents came together, it could best be described as the Bible says, "When the blind shall lead the blind, they both fall into the ditch." As it were they bought their first home in the ditch! They lived in the ditch of despair. They each had limited knowledge of what it meant to be a spouse. But they knew one thing they were supposed to do. That was to have children; and so they did.

First came my sister Rhonna, who is four years older than I. Then came yours truly, the middle child of the three. Two and a half years later my brother David was born, completing the family as it is today. Let me state without reservation, my parents did the best they could. Of course, they carried into their marriage and family the limitations and hurts from their past. They were so wrapped up in trying to survive, themselves. They struggled to create a family, never giving up or giving in. Everyone has something to overcome, and my parents deserve the congressional medal of survival! Eventually, praise God we all became Christians and moved ahead in our lives.

However, the early years of our upbringing makes the greatest impact. Those years are often filled with insecurity and immaturity and lead to the impartation of models for the next generation. In fact, behavioral scientists tell us that by about age 10, the self-concept is fully formed in children. By this age most children have a basic concept about who they are, what they are about, their feelings, their importance, their sense of worth or lack thereof. They have an internal perception of being loved or not and whether they are a good person or a bad apple.

All of that is established between ages 8 and 10. If one has teenagers who are having troubles, part of the reason for this is because they are teenagers and they are *possessed*. They are possessed with hormones! Not demon possessed! They have been kissed with the hormone fairy, which presents certain problems, which tag along with their condition. If one has a child that does not like itself a lot, it could be rooted in some of the things that happened or did not happen in their earlier upbringing. The important ingredients of a healthy childhood will be explored in detail later in this book. What is so very often seen is mom and dad coming together, trying to do the best they can, but because of unconscious destructive patterns, unknowingly creating or exacerbating problems for the very children they so desperately love.

## Personal Results/Responses

My family is very expressive. As a family, there were no subjects of discussion which were taboo. We knew about politics, religion and sex from an early age. We could yell and scream at each other, cuss, snort, spit and five minutes later do lunch. It was nothing personal. That is the kind of family we are. We intensely love each other, and intensely hate each other, but we stick together. So in our family, though there may have been tough times, we purposed to remain in some semblance of relationship.

## The Better Half!?

I have my issues and problems from my childhood. I am far from perfect. As time marched on, I came to "the marrying time" and fortunately for me met a lovely woman named Karen. She is a truly beautiful woman; a lovely lady. However, she comes from a different kind of family than mine.

Her family was one of the most silent families I've ever known in my life. A typical full day's conversation was "Good Morning", "Good Bye", "I'll see you when I get home", a kiss at the door when they came in "What's for dinner?", and "Good night!" They could go a whole day and never talk. I cannot seem to go three minutes! So of course, Karen and I met and I fell immediately into love (it took her a few weeks to be convinced). By the grace of God and my good fortune, we finally got married. We did not wait six weeks. We waited almost two years before marrying.

Karen was not born again when I first met her. I do not recommend this to most people. I'd surveyed the church, there were no good looking ladies, so... It is not a theological thing, but it worked. We have been married twenty-four years. Glory to God! That is almost a miracle nowadays. But it hasn't all been wedded bliss. We have caused each other significant trouble.

When we got married, I had one view of what married life was all about. She had an entirely different view. She came from a family that had gone through a divorce, and a very treacherous divorce at that. This left her with a deep sense of insecurity about relationships. I am very different in that way, much less insecure (at least on the surface) in relationships. The differences in our family of origin have created conflict for us in a number of different arenas.

Eventually, we had children. Rebecca was born June 1, 1976. What a wonderful day. She's a Georgia girl, born at Fort Benning. Rebecca is a true gift of God, as is our number one number two daughter, Rachel. Our life dramatically changed when Rebecca came into the world and changed even more radically when her sister Rachel was born.

I have a concept of parenting that is somewhat different than my wife's. My concept was very much hands on and directive. Hers was more hands off and non-directive. Neither was better than the other was, just different. When one parents, the most important issue is consistency and agreement. Many fine and effective parents are very, very easy. Some would say that they let their children get away with murder. But, they are very consistent and they do have boundaries. As long as the parenting is consistent, in agreement, the sternness or slackness is inconsequential.

The first step that a parent must take to become a purposeful parent is to recognize the dynamics that go into making up a set of parents. It is not just biology. It is not just what one knows or how one speaks to the children. Nor is it even discipline or limits are set. ***Parenting is an outgrowth of the relationship between a husband and wife***. The Bible, which is the Christian's authority for living says, "A man shall leave his father and mother, cleave to his wife and the two shall become one flesh" (Gen. 2:24). One of the conditions of a one-flesh relationship is to properly resolve family of origin issues and loyalties before marriage occurs. This rarely if ever happens, even with the best of pre-marital counseling. Once the leaving and cleaving occurs, then the result will be "They were naked and without shame." They were vulnerable to each other. In many marriages, this is not the case. Partners are unable to be vulnerable with each other, generally due to past hurt. There is much shame. That causes spouses to hide from each other. Thus, they are unable to come into agreement in many areas of life. This can be due to a fear of being hurt, thus the couple is not living in a one-flesh union, let alone with one spirit or purpose. Whenever there is a divided house, it sets the stage for many significant problems. One of the questions that counselors ask and must ensure as a foundation for good parenting is, are the parents singing off of the same sheet of music, do they have the maturity for marriage and family?

Children are not just clever, they are insidiously clever. They have a sixth sense when it comes to any type of disagreement between parents. They seem to know when there is division in the household. When they find even the slightest crack (it is not as though they want to divide and conquer), they must test it to see whether or not mom and dad are going to remain united. It is difficult to remain in unity as biological parents and even more so if a stepparent or single parent family system. The more people involved in the parenting process, the more room for division and the greater the need for good communication and unity. When one has both natural father and mother, stepfather, stepmother, grandparents, etc., one must establish a common ground of child rearing and discipline. It is well documented that parents should begin from a place of firmness and clear unity, based upon agreed upon principles, to be effective in the parenting process. Without this, there will be constant tension. A divide and conquer spirit will develop. For example, when a child has gone through the divorce of their parents, and a stepparent comes in, what would be their greatest fear? Divorce again. Of course, most children carry an internalized belief that they caused the breakup of their family or had some contributing factor in it. They determine that this must never happen again. Yet, they have to test the strength of the union. They have to bang against imposed limits to find out whether or not this new family will remain intact.

When one considers all of the dynamics that make up one's parenting style and family life, it is essential that unity be developed based upon living principles that are found in the Word of God.

Parenting is not a simple task. It is not an issue of biology. Parenting is not instinctive. What is learned in the family of origin, from society in general, and through friends encountered are not always the healthiest or helpful. Many models have been borrowed from watching television. Models such as the Brady Bunch, Ozzie and Harriet, (did Ozzie ever work?) the Bunker's, (that is closer to the reality of the modern American family, or even "Roseanne") which help to create images which swim around in the personal unconscious. For parenting to be successful, one must evaluate these learned patterns and perceptions, reviewing them for accuracy, so as to understand them more clearly. Those beliefs that are deemed false or destructive must be replaced with the truth that is found in God's word. With the word, and the natural wisdom gained through observation of human behavioral methods, Godly results can be gained.

## On Purpose

Purpose, in context of this teaching, is the art of understanding and utilizing God's Word as applied to the task of parenting. Believers who are parents must come to an understanding of what God's plan is, and then submit to His plan as a priority for their lives. This is true in every aspect of the Christian walk, but it is especially vital in parenting. One reason for this is that parenting is the first human institution ordained by God, and remains the best vehicle for the perpetuation of the race. When the Lord formed man from the dust, and later from a portion of the man's side, He did so with specific purpose. The purpose of God, as seen in Genesis 1:26-28, is that the image and likeness of God would be expanded throughout the whole earth, and that the man and woman would rule over all that God had created as co-equal partners. Some would proclaim that the purpose of God in the beginning has been completely thwarted by man's fall and the devil's dominion. However, the plans of God have not changed from the beginning. He still intends to raise up a Godly seed, a people within the earth who will rule with justice and mercy as the "parents of the earth". And He still intends to use mankind as the stewards of all He has created.[2]

Only God is the perfect parent. God desires for all of us to emulate him as parent in terms of our focus or purpose. God is invested in humanity becoming just like Him, which is impossible without His grace, mercy and the power of the Spirit operating in our lives. If mankind begins to act as the Father in all that they are doing, His requirements of parental stewardship will be satisfied. Unfortunately, even God in His perfection could not guarantee that His children would respond to the most loving parent in a positive way. Due to rebellion, mankind has inherent, passed on from generation to generation, the insidious sin nature. Inherited within every child is the ability to destroy the creative work of God, which is imparted by the best of loving parents. But, as one approaches the model of God the Father in the way that parenting is conducted, one can come closer and closer to fulfilling a major part of their destiny in God.

---

[2] The theme of rulership with Christ begins in Genesis, and continues through the book of Revelation. For example, in Romans 14:12, the Apostle Paul, echoing the Prophet Isaiah (11:1+) states that the purpose of the Lord, the mystery of God was that the Gentiles would come under the dominion o the Lordship of Christ. Thus, the Gentile would also inherit the blessings of Abraham if obedient, or the judgment of God if disobedient. Further, the saints of God would also rule with the Lord, in every aspect of life, as seen in II Tim. 2:12. One place where the purposes of God can be fulfilled is in the family.

*"...so that they may encourage the young women to love their husbands, to love their children."*

**Titus 2:4**

# Chapter 3

# The Word on Parenting

Let us look at some of the references in the word of God to parenting, with practical application. Genesis chapter 2 has already been presented in brief, but bears expansion for the purposes of this study. Genesis 2:24 says, "For this cause, a man shall leave his father and his mother and shall cleave to his wife and they shall become one flesh." The greatest difficulty in the parenting process is the result of either or both of the parents being unable to leave the family of origin, and subsequently cleave to one another. There must be a leaving before there can be a cleaving. Every individual carries certain character traits of their mother and father, their beliefs, attitudes and behaviors, into the new world of marriage and family. That is normal and natural. From what can be determined from the Bible, unless a certain belief, attitude or behavior is contrary to the Word of God, there's nothing specifically wrong with this. It is the way life develops. All of mankind learns from those who have gone before; like begets like.

However, there must be a conscious decision to let go of loyalty factors to mom and dad so one can cleave to the other. When it comes time to have a family, many prospective parents are tempted to call mommy or daddy, asking them for advice on parenting or other matters. Armed with this authoritative information, they apply it to their spouse regardless of how their spouse feels. This demonstrates to their spouse a loyalty to mom or dad, which is greater than to their own spouse. This can and often does undermine the relationship between the couple, causing resentment and division. Thus, a couple must leave and cleave. When done, this provides ample room for the Lord to begin to give new insights and biblical concepts for the marriage and family relationship. Leaving and cleaving is a necessary prerequisite to becoming one flesh, or establishing a unity and maturity necessary for effective parenting.

The scripture continues, "...*the man and his wife were both naked and where not ashamed.*" In context one will note that this scripture describes a time prior to the sin of Adam, also called the fall of man. When Christ died on the cross and His provision for salvation is received, it provides to all new life in the spirit of man. With this wonderful gift comes the potential ability to be as Adam was prior to the fall. As God views man, He sees through the cross of Christ, and the precious blood shed, thus He chooses to see man in light of a renewed spirit. God sees man as complete, whole, wonderful, as Adam was in the garden. Man is now a new creation in Christ, part of the second Adam. In the natural, most Christians do not see themselves with such a lofty esteem. The fact is, from the present reality of an earth bound view, the best of believers are not fully what God intends for them to be. But in terms of position and potential, man already is what God says that he is. Though most Christians are aware of and truly thankful to the Lord for their position in Christ, there remains the need to respond to life within one's present reality. There is reality and then there is reality. There is God's reality, which is that man is complete and holy in Christ, and there is *our* reality which is that all are being conformed to the image of Christ, being changed from glory to glory as each believer looks into the face of Christ. All believers, even in their failures, are growing into the likeness of God over time and through experience.

The ideal biblical perspective is that the husband and wife, when they get married, become physically, emotionally and spiritually transparent, without barriers or boundaries between each other. Thus, they can share each other's person with an openness and honesty, and build on a fresh biblical foundation.

In American culture, there is a time of great openness, usually in the very beginning of the relationship. This is a magical time, filled with hopes, dreams and expectations of wedded bliss. It is sometimes helpful for couples to remember when the courtship first began. Most couples were totally in love, fully infatuated with one another, thoroughly enveloped in the feelings of love. Essentially, love is deaf, dumb, blind and stupid! That is, in the beginning of most relationships which are characterized by a strong romantic attachment, one could not see any faults in the partner, and if any were seen, they would be immediately dismissed them as irrelevant. Why? Because of the intense feeling of love experienced, a most marvelous but deceptive state! That is brain damage! The fact is it is most difficult to see things clearly when the eyes of understanding are closed, and when the eyes being viewed through are clouded with profound and blissful emotions. That is why, even with the best of pre-marital counseling, that most couples blindly believe that their marriage will be without fault, full and simply marvelously, living happily ever after. Oh how I wish it were true.

One of the reasons for the incomplete and jaded beginning of most relationships is that many couples start out as liars. It is not a malicious lie, but a purposeful one. Neither the man nor the woman in a dating relationship wants rejection, so they put their best foot forward. Few, if any, couples started their dating experience by picking an available nose on the first date. However, it is highly doubtful that the finding of the nose for the purposes of finger insertion is not accomplished shortly after marriage. A young suitor would never think of showing up to a lovely ladies house unshaven, even on Saturday morning. Saturday may be a no shave day but not while dating unless it is the "macho I am a studmuffin" look of the week! Never would the young lady be seen with curlers in her hair until after marriage. Then of course all bets are off. So, most couples start out as liars and then attempt to become honest later. This course of action is generally forgiven as the ritual deception is seemingly required to catch the perfect match. However, the down side of this is that once the truth becomes painfully known, there can be shock and dismay.

Usually by the time one starts really learning about each other, they have already developed a certain amount of defenses against each other. Those defenses can become barriers or strongholds in the relationship, which will no doubt cause difficulty down the road. To further complicate matters, many parents have not had a naked and unashamed time. That is, though the physical expression of vulnerability (nakedness) has been expressed, the emotional part, longed for to a greater or lesser dimension by both in the marriage, has yet to be shared. This can occur for several reasons, including pre-mature physical relations (often, sex can be the greatest barrier to health openness, and used as an avoidance for true intimacy), immaturity in the relationship (self-centered need gratification, control, etc.) or psychological wounds from past relationships which are carried into the existing one. These barriers should be removed prior to saying " I do", but this unfortunately is rarely the case.

Healthy love relationships are based on friendships that lead to deep commitment, eventually becoming romantic and sexually expressed (in marriage). When this happens, couples build on a foundation of mutual encouragement and support because they already know each other well. They have seen each other at their worst and are mature enough to be able to work through conflicts with grace. In other words, they have worked out the "dance steps" of their relationship together. Unfortunately, most relationships do not begin with a solid foundation. Barriers develop as self-protecting mechanisms that can severely disrupt the relationship and need gratification.

Being a couple can be difficult enough, let alone a parent. In healthy homes, a new child becomes a joyful expression of the couples love and devotion to one another. However, in less functional relationships, the baby can become one or the other parents' primary relationship. Usually, if they have a second child, a split in the attention towards the children will occur. In this scenario, one parent will focus time and attention on one child; where as the other child receives the attention of the other parent. Thus one will have mom's child and dad's child. This split, if it occurs (and many are not total splits, but often there is a switching back and forth, or the split can be to a greater or lesser degree) they will function that way for the next twenty years. If there's a third child, often one will find he or she becoming a lost child. In some cases the middle child may become the lost child, becoming displaced by the new baby in the family.

More often than not the dad will primarily bond with a daughter and mom with a son. When this tragic change in the primary relationship occurs (the husband-wife relationship)[3], for the next twenty-five years or so the parents will lead parallel lives, separated under the same roof in terms of communication and overall focus of attention. Dad works, which is where he receives most of his emotional needs met, and secondarily has his need for communication met through his son or daughter. At the same time, mom functions in the primary role of mother, only secondarily as wife, and meets some of her communicative needs through one of the children. Eventually, if the marriage survives the loneliness, they may attempt to reestablish their relationship, but generally find this to be extremely difficult. They do not even know each other. If they are unable to reestablish a relationship (usually this bridging of the relationship occurs during the mid-life transition of the man), they may divorce, or begin to vicariously live out their life through their grandchildren. And the beat goes on!

This is not God's plan. God's plan is naked and unashamed. That is, a relationship based upon mutual knowledge and trust in one another, communications without need for secrecy, mutual respect and vulnerability. Then when children are born to this union, it is based upon a common agreement and an expression of each other's and God's love. Ideally, all children should be brought into a world filled with the love of two parents. Too often parents will have children because they know that

---

[3] For a more extensive study on the relationship priorities mandated in the Word of God, see *Marriage and Family Life: A Christian Perspective* also by this author.

their children have to love <u>them</u>. One should not be too surprised by this. Most of the readers of this book either know people like this, or are the very same people looked at in the mirror in the morning! That does not mean one cannot change. God is the change agent. If a parent realizes that they have looked to their child to love them instead of loving the child without conditions (to the best of their ability, no one is perfect), they do not have to be disillusioned, disappointed and discouraged. It is always possible to turn things around with God's help and a full understanding of His plan.

It will take courage and the power of the Holy Spirit to implement a new plan. It is never too late.

## The Way the Cookie Crumbles

All of the dynamics discussed above (and probably many others, which are lesser in severity and importance) go into the making of a parent. If there is conflict between mom and dad, it will be played out in some form through the pressure of parenting when the children come along. For example, when Johnny comes running up and says, "Mom, can I have a cookie?" Mom says, "No, you can't have a cookie, it is going to spoil your dinner." "But mom." "I said No!" Dad's home. Johnny goes to dad. "Dad, oh great man, oh fine provider, you've just come home from the wars and I know you are such a man. Can I have a cookie?" "Son, young man of my loins, of course! Take two. For you are just like me, <u>obnoxious</u>." Then of course, mom finds out. Mom says, "I told him no!" Dad says, "Yes, but he's a growing boy, he needs his cookies." And in many cases, they are off to the races, amplifying this simple conflict into a mountainous disagreement or argument.

Over time, these tiny, seemingly insignificant situations become major areas of conflict. Parents must work to be in agreement. In this example, the parents are not being faithful over little. Thus, when the big issues come, they will likely have a divided camp, making agreement for the benefit of all concerned most difficult. God's intention is for the husband and wife to be in agreement about parenting, even in the small things.

In the beginning of our parenting (which has been far from perfect) my wife and I agreed that if one child asked one parent for something and then went to the other parent, we would check with each other. That very simple rule between judiciously followed has saved us much heartache. Our goal had been to make sure that our children received nothing through manipulation and thus enjoyed the security of a united front. In other words, we determined to stay united in our treatment of the children, for their benefit and for our peace of mind. That way, they could not divide and conquer us, which would have created a sense of insecurity for the children and potential mistrust for us as parents. When children are allowed to divide and conquer, it causes great tension. This results in feelings of insecurity and causes them to continue to test in the same areas. Further, it can cause bitterness and resentment within the relationship.

## Doing It God's Way

Deuteronomy 6 provides for the parent a picture of God's Plan in parenting. It is one of the most profound passages in the word of God having to do with parenting and the parenting process. Deuteronomy 6:1 says, "Now this is the commandment, the statutes and the judgments which the Lord your God has commanded me to teach you. That you might do well in the land where you are going over to possess it." The Lord is primarily talking about the Ten Commandments. These are the laws that were presented by God to Moses to give to the people. Now again, hear what this says, in my paraphrased version. "The commandments, the statutes, the judgments which the Lord God has commanded to teach or impart are to be listened to and followed with a sincere devotion. The focus or purposes of these teachings are to prepare my people for inheriting the promises that have been previously stated, and are summarized here. There are possessions that are to be possessed by the people of God, and all that is required to do so is obedience to the commandments that have been taught."

Here is something very important to remember. God has possessions for His people to possess. Obadiah verse 17 states that in Judah, *"there would be a people who would possess their possessions."* This is talking about a future people. There has been many a prophetic message spoken over the pulpits of the church that the day has come for God's people to begin to inherit the promises of God. Many national leaders recognize that the church is in a season where their is a greater understanding of just what the kingdom of God is, and that God is imparting and empowering His people to possess the promises found in His word. Thus, there has been a focus of attention on doing spiritual warfare to possess the land that God has given. Of course, it is always easier to fight an enemy that is not easily seen. Unfortunately the greatest battleground for spiritual warfare is often in the very familiar family which we live in.

Whether it is in a church or a community, the focus of the Lord has always been to possess the possession[4] of a healthy family. Strong families, which begin with strong marriages, are the foundation for a strong church and a strong society. Fragmented families, lacking a common purpose are impotent to change the world. The church must have united families if the possession of the promises of the Lord is to be achieved. It is required for the purposes of God to be fulfilled, that parents listen to and obey the commandments of the Lord, and follow them faithfully.

In the passage presented above, Moses was speaking about actual land and real warfare to possess it. From a New Testament viewpoint, land means more than just geography. It is speaking about every promise found in the word of God that pertains to His children. If God has provided a husband or given a wife, even though at times one might like to give them back, they're still a precious possession, a gift from the Lord. Once received, one becomes responsible for the proper care of the gracious gift. Children are a gift from God, and part of ones "possession". They are part of the family inheritance. God wants parents to "possess" them, "So that you and your son and your grandson might fear the Lord your God." "The fear of God is the beginning of wisdom and knowledge." (Ps. 111:10)

One of the purposes for obeying the commandments of the Lord is so that respect will be built into one's children. It is a well-documented fact that it is vital for children to learn basic respect for legitimate authority at an early age. Respect really has to do with the fear or the awe and reverence of the Lord. How do children learn this reverence? By learning to reverence their parents. One of the ways my wife and I have jokingly expressed this to our children has been to tell them, "Remember, to obey

---

[4] What is meant by possession in the Old Testament is often quite different than the New Testament concept or the modern day notions. In ancient Israel, the Hebrews were quite a barbaric race, and women and children were often treated as nothing more than cattle or another prize animal. The principal presented here is one of taking responsibility for a precious gift, not one of ownership. Wives are not the chattel of property of the man, to be used and discarded at will or whim, nor are children to be treated without a view towards respect and nurture, a primary New Testament concept which will be explored in greater depth later. For more on this, see Dr. Ken Chant's work on Hermeneutics in **_Understanding the Bible._**

is better then being sacrificed!" The Word of God says that worship with the lips is nothing compared to worship from the heart that is demonstrated by obedience to God's commandments. Children learn to worship the Lord by having a basic respect for parents and subsequently for the Lord.

A parent's primary goal should be that their children learn to fear the Lord. One of the things that is missing in Western society is a respect for right and wrong. There is an abysmal lack of a basic sense of law and order, which comes from a lack of respect for proper authority, including parental authority. The reaction to lawlessness in society has been to build bigger prisons that are structured for punishment. A parent's focus should be on providing resources to their children so they can be properly trained, rather than voting for more money to build prisons for those who have not learned respect or are reaping a harvest from sown abuse and neglect. There must be a renewed commitment to the equipping of parents to effectively rear their children. This is the hope for the future of every nation.

The plan and purpose of God is that children (adults as well) might fear the Lord and respect His Word. Often a demand is placed on children to respect adults, and if they do not they are punished. The expectation is that little children give absolute obedience and allegiance to the parents every whim and command.

In truth, children love to show honor and respect to their parents. It is natural for them to want to obey and please them. What causes most children to begin the disobedience process is not demons, nor is it even the old nature in most cases. It is usually discouragement. This discouragement will be discussed in detail later, but first more on the commandments of God.

Referring back to Deuteronomy 6 it says, *"Keep all his statutes and his commandments which I command you all the days of your life, that your days may be prolonged."* How many parents want to see their children live to a ripe old age? Jesus may come back soon yet, until He comes, His church and all His people are to be actively in the process of church building. The family, as the foundation of the church, is to be active in helping the next generation to see the *"goodness of the Lord in the land of the living"* (Psalms 27:13). Part of the responsibility of parents in this generation is to prepare the responsible adults for the next generation. No longer can members live for today with the idea that Jesus is coming back to rescue them from this miserable world, thus having no responsibility for the future. Christians have and always will have a responsibility for the future generation.

The Lord wants His children to keep all of His statutes that the life of the believer might be prolonged as would the children's. Then it says, *"Oh, Israel you should listen and be careful to do it. That it may be well with you and that you may multiply greatly just as the Lord the God of your fathers has promised you in a land flowing with milk and honey."* What a wonderful promise from the Father.

> Verse 4 says, *"Hear Oh Israel, the Lord is our God, the Lord is one. And you shall love the Lord your God with all your heart, with all your soul and with all your might. These words which I am commanding you today, shall be in your heart. And you shall teach them diligently to your sons, to your daughters, and shall talk of them when you sit in your house, when you walk by the way and when you lie down and when you rise up. And you shall bind them on as a sign on your hand, and they shall be as frontlets on your forehead and you shall write them on the doorpost of your house and on your gates."*

God's intention is for the believer is that they be fruitful in all areas of their lives, especially in family life. To see this promise come to pass, is to hear and understand the Lord and His purposes, and act on these purposes, especially and primarily when the children are young. If the love of God is the central focus of ones heart, soul, mind and strength, and the love of neighbor as oneself, and if these principles are taught to ones children, the parents will see from this sowing a positive, abundant harvest. The teaching of these principles must be repeated over and over and over again to become a part of a child's lifestyle. Essentially, what children will learn and emulate comes from the themes that the parents act upon on a consistent basis, less by what a parent says than by what is demonstrated daily.

As stated above, marriage is the foundation for family life. God's purpose is to indoctrinate His people into His Word and incorporate His principles and concepts into their lives. With this indoctrination will come the ability or power to model to one's children a Godly lifestyle. Thus, they will learn the fear of the Lord or the respect of God and His authority, by seeing the same principles acted out and discussed by observation in the parents. Of course, this is the ideal, no one does it perfectly; no one ever will.

As a parent teaches by example and word, children learn a balanced respect for legitimate authority. Many adults who were raised in the fifties and sixties, before all of the craziness of the "Me" generation, had parents that were very concerned about what others thought. They taught such things as not to walk across somebody's yard, not to touch somebody's car, never to take someone else's possessions. If a child of the 50's and early 60's took something from a local store, they were marched back to the store, made to apologize, so as to set things right. Unfortunately, that is an era gone by. Beginning in the mid-sixties, the parenting style changed, much of it influenced by Dr. Benjamin Spock and the interpretation of his writings. (Some of what he wrote was actually quite good and most practical). To paraphrase with prejudice his primary philosophy, children were to be seen as wonderful creatures, by nature good. The belief was that to correct or punish a child would damage their budding self-image. Encouraged by this philosophy, and the guilt placed upon parents who went against the philosophy of the day, parents allowed their children to do whatever they wanted, with the assumption that they would naturally grow to be wonderful responsible adults. In the seventies, with drugs, "do your own thing" and "nobody can tell me what to do", the restraints were removed and authority disregarded. This has produced the fruit of today's parenting style, and much of the disintegration of moral national values. Evangelical churches have reacted to the liberal, permissive parental style in an opposite direction. In reaction to the more permissive philosophy of do not disciple children, many Christians have gone the other way; disciplining their children for everything! Discipline defined by many as the right and need to punish, not the biblical mandate to train and teach. The scripture states that parents are to train and teach in the morning, during the day, at night, as they walk along the way. Meaning, it is in the precious yet common daily interactions of life, played out over time and experience that provide the greatest opportunity to teach children the important issues of life. The very things that are emphasized by the parents will become the important items of emphasis to the children as they mature.

## Train and Teach

Proverbs 22:6 is a very famous and often quoted by parents with wayward children passage of scripture. The verse reads, *"Train up a child in the way he should go, even when he is old, he will not depart from it."* Some have used this passage as a proof that their child will become born again, but this is not its meaning within proper biblical context.

A better interpretation would be that whatever a parent programs into a child when they are young will eventually be seen in the children. In other words, when they become adults, they will tend to repeat what they have learned within the family of origin. They will follow and do the same things that they have seen their parents do. What a frightening thought! This is why behaviors from the past are often repeated in the children's present. When children reach maturity, they are not going to depart from what they've learned as children. Thus, it is most important to train children in such a way that they will grow to maturity, becoming responsible, functional adults.

Now notice it says, *"Train up a child."* Parents are to train young children, but teach older children and adults. A definition by way of illustration may be in order. If a parent is going to attempt to teach a four-year-old, they will become extremely frustrated. Teaching is a didactic process literally meaning to impart information to that individual so that they can then act upon it. Four-year-olds do not act upon what they hear; they act upon what they feel or what has been demonstrated to them.

## A Training Example

If you have a four or five-year-old child, and you want to train them how to take a bath, you certainly would not have them sit down on the couch with you sitting across from them and explain to them the importance of cleanliness. If you attempted this, as parents often do, you might say, "Now, you do understand what your peers are going to think if you stink. It is very important that you take a shower at least three times a week because body odor is bad, you could get germs, etc." How long will it take into that conversation before the child is picking lint out of his navel? They are not going to hear a word being said. If it were time to instruct a child on how to take a bath, the most effective method would be to simply take the child by the wrist and say, "let's go." Taking them by the hand, the parent leads the precious child to the bathtub, helping them out of their clothes, while simultaneously filling the tub with appropriately warm water, putting them in the tub and assisting them in the washing ritual. The child is rarely consulted in this process, nor should they be. This is how to train them in this important life skill. The parent might state as they lead in the training "Here you put soap on the washcloth, then you begin to wash, etc." As the parent leads, they begin to "learn" what is demonstrated to them.

What happens in many families is that some training happens when children are very young, but eventually the exhausted parents run out of energy. This is especially true when a second child arrives and the first one is still in diapers. The parental priority naturally shifts from the first child to the second, while the first child has to move ahead on their merry way, attempting to figure out how to live life with limited guidance. Thus, parents often end the training process too soon. This problem, that of not being able to complete the training aspect of children, is made worse when there is an absent or ineffectual father in the home, when illness occurs, etc. There is a certain amount of training that will continue until they leave home, but it becomes less training and more teaching.

## A Shifting

A shift needs to begin at approximately age 8-10, from simple concrete teaching (do this because I said so), to teaching (do this for a legitimate reason, or abstract reasoning). Ultimately, we want to teach teens (about ages 13-21) principles from God's Word which will sustain them throughout their life. Further, the teaching of adult responsibilities like banking, car maintenance, how to write a check, make a deposit, etc., must also be imparted to the young adults. They must learn to function responsibly as adults.

There are many other consumer skills that must be taught. How many young women (or even men for that matter) know how to change a tire, change the oil, or put gas in a car? They have never been trained to do any of these consumer behaviors. This often results in an inability to function fully in a rapidly changing society, ignorant as to how to live life on a daily basis without being taken unfair advantage of. It is a parent's responsibility to continue to train so that the young person can be fully functional as an adult when they are on their own. Even in the financial area, a parent can help the young adult. This can be accomplished by assisting them to obtain a debit card. A debit card allows for a certain amount of money to be placed on account. The young person is only allowed to charge up to what is in the account. This teaches them faithfulness and proper management of credit. The reality is, if the young person is taught how to manage credit well when they are young, they are less likely to have to come back to mom and dad for a bail out of their financial problems. Thus, it is a good investment.

There will always be a certain amount of training for children. Again the Word says, *"Train a child and when they are old, they will not depart from what they have learned through that training process."*, whether good or bad. If a parent has trained their child to avoid conflict, they will learn to avoid conflict. If they have been trained to deal with things directly, they will learn to be problem solvers. Whatever the model that has been presented tends to be what they will repeat in future generations.

*"Children obey your parents in the Lord for this is right."*

**Ephesians 6:1**

# Chapter 4

## The Word on Disciplining

In Proverbs 23:13 it says, *"Do not hold back discipline from the child. Although you beat him with the rod, he will not die."* Most parents say, Amen! Verse 14 continues *"You shall beat him with the rod and deliver his soul from hell."* Also Prov. 13:24 says, *"He who spares his rod, hates his son. But he who loves him, disciplines him diligently."* Then Prov. 22:15 says, *"Foolishness is bound up in the heart of a child, the rod of discipline will remove it far from him."* Another, Prov. 26:3 says, *"The rod of correction is for the back of a fool."*

Many have read these scriptures and have gained from it that it is very important for parents to punish one's children with spankings. How many parents have been taught this? How many present day parents were raised in the same fashion? Most Christian parents have become convinced that physical discipline is the most important form of discipline for a child. Well, it certainly has its place, but must be kept in proper biblical perspective. The word <u>rod</u> in Hebrew means correction or discipline. If a parent withholds discipline (discipline means to train or teach), if a child is not taught or trained in right living, they will be spoiled.

In the reference above where it says, *"The rod of correction is for the backside of a fool,"* it is in that case a literal rod. But it is for the back of a fool or one who is in absolute rebellion against authority. It was one step away from taking them to the edge of the city and stoning them to death. There was an example of this not too long ago, as seen in the in the young man who was punished in Singapore. Everyone who visits that country knows that they have some very rigid rules. Some of their rules seem strange to the mind of an American. For instance, one can actually receive a five hundred-dollar fine if they fail to flush their toilet. This young man should have known about the possible consequences of violating their laws. Unfortunately for the young man, he was apparently a typical arrogant American. He must have determined that he would not get caught desecrating property and if they did he would just say he was an American and they would let him go. I am sure he learned, as have all foreigners entering Singapore, that whether the rules seem right or wrong they will be enforced, and swift punishment of the "rod" if one is convicted of being a fool will be administered.

As a father, I would not want my child to receive a beating, but I hope my child would not be doing something that would necessitate such discipline. Absolute rebellion against known authority is foolish and demands a strong response. Even the eminent psychologist James Dobson agrees that defiance deserves a strong parental reaction. Absolute defiance against legitimate authority deserves physical correction because there appears to be a direct nerve connection from the buttocks to the brain. However, only if it is clearly rebellious defiance, not mistakes, should such severe discipline be given. Most of what children are corrected for with physical discipline is for behavioral mistakes, or is out of their own frustration. How this occurs and what can be done to correct an inappropriate response will be explored in detail later. The tragic fact is that parents can unknowingly teach negative and destructively violent patterns when physical correction is poorly and inappropriately administered.

Now, let's look at two more passages of scripture. Mark 10:13 presents Jesus blessing the little children. Through these scriptures one can see a clear picture of God's plan and purpose. Verse 13 says, *"And when they were bringing children to him so that he might touch them, and the disciples rebuked them."* Obviously, Jesus was enjoying himself. He was more then welcoming to the children and gladly received them.

This was probably not the first time this had occurred, and was most likely a common custom of Jesus. It was not common for Rabbi's or master teachers to touch children or have much to say or do regarding their care. As is true in the vast majority of cultures today, parenting was the active responsibility of the mother. Mom's dealt with children, dads were occupied with philosophical hyperbole. In the passage of scripture referred to above, Jesus is breaking an old model and establishing a new pattern and priority. The new model can be summarized in the statement, "When Jesus saw this, he was indignant." He wasn't ignorant. He was angry. He was most disappointed at his disciples' lack of sensitivity and awareness of Kingdom priorities. How dare they stop what Jesus was doing? The disciples were missing the whole point. Their primary responsibility was to watch Jesus, observing His way of operation, so that in the future the disciples could repeat similar patterns. The disciples appeared to be more concerned with image, as it were a political/religious correctness than to see the fulfillment of the purposes of God.

Essentially, Jesus was modeling what discipleship is all about, and further what attitude towards children is required for parenting on purpose to be effective. Most parents would love to have their children follow their positive patterns, and emulate them in the future. If a parents' focus has been to have their children not to become like they are, there must come a shift in thinking. Many parents carry in their mind a defensive, negative, resistant posture. Rather, parents need to declare, "I want to be the kind of person that would be pleasing to God so that my children will follow me, and thus their lives will be much better than mine." What a vastly different paradigm (belief system that one operates from) shift this is. This modified form of thinking will most certainly change their perception of their role as parents. In other words, if one is able to parent with a purpose, they must be willing to change.

Jesus goes on to say (in the authors paraphrased version), "permit the children to come to me, do not stop them, allow them to keep coming. Do not hinder them, for the kingdom of God belongs to such as these." In Jesus' teaching he is saying to them, look, you need to see children from a different light. Do not view them as little more than a nuisance to the work of God. But see them as I see them; see them as the Father sees them. Children are what the Kingdom is all about. These children are precious, important, to be loved, nurtured and of course as parents, one's ultimate responsibility is to bring children to Jesus, never to hinder them. The greatest hope for all mankind is to learn from the parent of all parents, God the Father as demonstrated through Jesus Christ.

## The Blockage

An unfortunate truth is that the inconsistent lifestyles of the average Christian (and more tragically, many spiritual leaders) actually hinders peoples desire to know the Lord. Just as children look at parents as God-like figures, so they look at their parents' behavior in church versus home. Where inconsistency is consistent, the child must decide which is real. Generally, they will believe the parents' action more than the words. Also, children observe their pastors and other leaders in the church, seen as surrogate fathers and mothers, second only to God Himself. For this reason, it is vital to encourage consistent patterns in parenting and in ministry to children, to provide proper care for the emotional and spiritual needs of the child. Children's programs are not developed so that the parents will attend church, undisturbed. The ministry to children, conducted within the local church, and their care is the primary focus of parenting on purpose.

Jesus continues his instruction "Let them come for the kingdom is as such as these. Truly I say to you, 'whoever does not receive the kingdom of God like a child shall not enter at all." Then it says, "And he took them in his arms and began blessing them, laying his hands on them." Jesus was comfortable enough with himself and with children to touch them in loving ways. Children need to be touched, they need to be loved, and they need to be included. Jesus modeled this loving affection towards children so His disciples and subsequently all of His followers throughout the ages would follow His pattern. It is through loving, appropriate touch, which affirms and builds the self-esteem of children.

**Inclusion**

I remember many, many times, observing our children as they would sit amongst the adults as conversations were occurring. Some of the other parents would become somewhat annoyed when I allowed their presence. My children would merely sit, saying nothing. But occasionally we would observe them becoming noticeably giddy and excited. It wasn't because they understood what was going on, they generally had no clue. The giddy joy of childhood manifested because they were included in the family circle. This made them feel very, very significant and worthwhile, setting in motion the learning process of relating in the adult world.

They belonged. One of the greatest needs in society is a sense of belonging. Often church life segments or divides children from their parents. This model did not exist until the 1960's. If one were to review history, churches had Sunday school programs that were evangelistic outreaches, generally held on Saturdays. They started with the Salvation Army as outreaches to children. Up until then, families came to church as a unit. Children learned to behave in church from mom and dad, who were right there with them. If a child was crying or acting in a disobedient fashion, they were carried outside for attention. When the crying was over, the parents would bring him or her back to join the family and the family of God. In theory, Children's Church programs have their place. They are excellent for outreach purposes as well as for parents that are unable to care for their children, or are seeking God themselves. For the rest of the body of Christ, it would be most appropriate to mature enough to take greater responsibility for the care of the precious children.

## Another Example

Whenever we were invited to visit a couple who said, "by the way we really do not want the children to come," we would politely excuse ourselves from the event. Except for special occasions, if the children were not welcome, we did not go. Sometimes parents need to be out on their own, but as much as possible, the children need to understand that they are of high priority to their parents. If gain a proper sense of their importance, not omnipotence (it must be in balance), there are much fewer problems with them in the future. Jesus was providing to our generation a model to follow. Children should be cared for. Include them, bless them, and put loving hands all over them. Make them feel loved, warm and special. It pays great dividends, but it does not matter if it pays a dividend, do it because the Father loves them, and out of obedience to the Lord and His word.

## Another Passage

Paul teaches, repeated in more than one place, the importance of marriage and family life. A brief review of the key passage from the book of Ephesians (5:22-33) will provide his very important slant on this most important issue.

Paul is writing to a Greek church that most assuredly did not have the foundation of faith as expounded in the Old Testament canon, the law and the prophets. He is writing to men and women with a philosophical/cultural belief system that reduced the worth of children, and treated the function of parenting as a necessary evil. As Greeks, they had been raised with humanistic, Hellenistic and materialistic models of rampant infidelity and easy divorce. Broken homes were the norm, child sexual exploitation common. Paul emphasized in his writing the importance of biblical models, teaching the importance of husbands loving their wives, wives submitting to their husbands, showing respect and honor to one another. He also speaks to the needs of children. But first, the whole teaching in proper context will be most helpful to a full understanding.

> *"Wives, be subject to your own husbands, as to the Lord. For the husband is the head of the wife, as Christ also is the head of the church, he Himself being the Savior of the body. But as the church*

> *is subject to Christ, so also the wives ought to be to their husbands in everything. Husbands, love your wives, just as Christ also loved the church and gave Himself up for her; that He might sanctify her, having cleansed her by the washing of water with the word, that He might present to Himself the church in all her glory, having no spot or wrinkle or any such thing; but that she should be holy and blameless. So husbands ought also to love their own wives as their own bodies. He who loves his own wife loves himself; for no one ever hated his own flesh, but nourishes and cherishes it, just as Christ also does the church, because we are members of His body. 31 For THIS CAUSE A MAN SHALL LEAVE HIS FATHER AND MOTHER, AND SHALL CLEAVE TO HIS WIFE; AND THE TWO SHALL BECOME ONE FLESH. This mystery is great; but I am speaking with reference to Christ and the church. Nevertheless let each individual among you also love his wife even as himself; and let the wife see to it that she respect her husband. Children, obey your parents in the Lord, for this is right. HONOR YOUR FATHER AND MOTHER (which is the first commandment with a promise), THAT IT MAY BE WELL WITH YOU, AND THAT YOU MAY LIVE LONG ON THE EARTH. And fathers, do not provoke your children to anger; but bring them up in the discipline and instruction of the Lord."* (Eph. 5: 22-6:4, NAS)

Even a cursory review of this passage tells the church of the importance of the family in God's economy. The care for children flows from the heart and purposes of the Lord Jesus through the parents (who hopefully are living in a healthy relationship with one another) to the children. More will be said about the parents later. For now the focus is on the children.

Chapter 6:1 says, *"Children obey your parents in the Lord for this is right."* It is right for children to obey their parents, a task that must be learned from an early age. Again, to obey is better than sacrifice. All of one's burnt offerings, all the time put into church, all the money given to charity does not matter unless one is obedient to the Word of God. Therefore, parents are to teach one's children to obey. But recognize, it is not easy for children to obey when the rules are either inconsistent or parents are unreasonable, especially in light of their developmental skills. If a parent were to ask a seven-year-old to do a certain task that is beyond their capability, the child will become discouraged. The children will either quit or not do what is requested because they are not capable of the task.

When children are asked, or urged, to function above their ability, and the children exhibit an inability to do so, parents often react by saying, "I told you to do it," and deal with the child as if they have a discipline problem, when most likely they do not. If a child is not developmentally ready, has not been properly trained to be able to do what they are asked, he or she will learn discouragement and failure, anger and resentment. Parents may assume that the child knows what they are saying and the meaning of the message or request. That is not a good assumption. Parents must ensure that they communicate with their children clearly, so that they will understand what's expected. Further, the parent should also see to it that their child has the capability of doing what is requested. If they know what's expected, and they are developmentally able to accomplish the task, and it is reasonable, one can reasonably assume that the child should and will obey. If they do not, then it may become a discipline problem, which will have to be addressed. The topic of discipline will be discussed in great detail later in this volume.

The Bible says, "*Honor your father and mother, which is the first commandment with promise.*" To honor means to show due respect. Children must learn to show their parents and all caring adults, the respect that is due them. For example, as I teach, I share stories about my mom and dad. They know what the stories are and have given me permission to share. If my mom and dad were to walk into a seminar of mine, I would still share the same stories and they would laugh right along with everyone else. I would never introduce them as the "two crazy folks that I lived with." I would introduce them by saying, this is my father, his name is Ron, and this is my mother, her name is Louise. I would honor them as my parents and speak of them with a positive sense of pride. I love and admire them for the people they are and for the fact that they are my parents.

This does not mean that I approved of or am happy about everything that they did. It does not mean that I feel good about all the decisions they made in terms of their discipline of me when I was a child; I do not. Many times their discipline was inappropriately applied. The wrong committed was done out of ignorance, not out of maliciousness. Having dealt with the past years ago, with ample forgiveness allowed, we love each other now more than ever. I will always honor them, for in spite of what has happened in the past, or may occur in the future, they still deserve honor.

In doing so, I become eligible to receive God's promise for me and help establish a positive role model for the next generation.

## Pass it On

All parents must teach their children that a person has a right to express their feelings, but must learn to do so with respect. It is alarming how many children do not know how to introduce their mother or father publicly. They have never learned how to properly address other adults or children. If one lives in the South, from Texas on, in the area of the United States known as the Bible belt, every little boy and girl knows exactly how to introduce their parents. They use yes ma'am, no ma'am, and yes sir, no sir. They are taught that respect is expected. Showing such respect to an elder is a core value of the culture, and a primary component of their lifestyle.

Of course, families from the South can be as dysfunctional as families from any other part of the country, sometimes worse. But, they do have a basic understanding of respect and honor. The system of respect sets the stage for true love to develop. Respect is the foundation of true love. God wants all adults and children to, "show honor to our parents, that it may be well with you and that you may live long on the earth."

Then the passage addresses fathers. When it says fathers, it is not just speaking about the biological father. It can be mothers as well, or any adult in a position of authority or influence in a child's life. *"Fathers do not exasperate your children; instead, bring them up in the training and instruction of the Lord"* (Eph. 6:4 NIV). In Col. 3:21 it says, *"Fathers do not embitter your children, or they will become discouraged."*

Parents provoke their children to anger when they have either asked them to do something that they are not capable of doing or have set an expectation on them that is too great for them to handle. This creates initial frustration, leading to anger.

Children become easily frustrated. Children will express anger because they are children. Exasperation is not the normal frustration that children and teenagers experience. The type of anger which leads to discouragement (internalized, unresolved anger and hurt), can be created when parents lay trips on their children, requiring them to do things they are not capable of. Another way in which parents can discourage their children is to force them to live up to certain standards that are impossible for them to achieve. When parents' lack understanding about the specific needs of their child, in terms of their place and time of life, (such as the importance of peer relationships during the teen years) the stage is set for acted out anger often called rebellion.

In some cases parents will provoke their children to anger by knowingly or unknowingly violating their natural boundaries. For instance, a child who is physically or otherwise abused experiences a tremendous violation of boundaries. The child is rightfully going to be angry. Since children do not know how to respond to parental abuse, they tend to internalize its message of rejection and betrayal, becoming discouraged, living in denial and ultimately facing a life of depression or other symptoms. These symptoms generally require significant pastoral care and counseling. Thus, fathers or parents must be careful not to discourage their children. Conversely, children are to be raised in the nurture and admonition of the Lord (Eph. 6:4). This means to provide, to the best of ones ability, unconditional love and discipline. These two key components of parenting on purpose will be discussed in detail in a later section.

The goal of all parenting is to raise a child to be mature enough as adults to respond to life as responsible citizens. Maturity includes the ability to delay ones gratification, work towards greater goals, be other oriented rather than self-absorbed, etc.

In order for parents to establish patterns of maturity in their children, it requires a concerted effort, provided over time and according to the developmental needs of the child, as discussed in the next chapter.

*"These words which I am commanding you today, shall be in your heart. And you shall teach them diligently to your sons, to your daughters, and shall talk of them when you sit in your house, when you walk by the way and when you lie down and when you rise up."*

**Deuteronomy 6:6-7**

# Chapter 5

# Purposeful Discipline

### Clear Expectation

It will help in the discussion to provide an example common in most homes, such as the task of taking out the trash. Many parents have attempted by bribery and threat to get their children to take out the trash. It is not a gift that most children have. Why do parents want their children to take out the trash? Because they do not want to do it! Because most parents (including yours truly) were made to do it as children. So, seeing that this one task is universal for all unhappy childhood chores, it is a worthy example for illustration.

A parent has decided to give their eight-year-old this task. Because parents are both intelligent and wise, they will not assume that the child knows what is meant by the request that they take out the trash. So the parent will make sure that they <u>train</u> and <u>teach</u> them the requirements of the task. This would begin by taking the child to each bedroom, after first stopping by the pantry to get a trash bag. Then, going from room to room, the child is shown how to dump the smaller trash into the larger trash bag, making sure they put the individual bedroom trash receptacles back where originally found. Then the parent and child will come to the kitchen where most people have their primary trash, and they dump all of the accumulated trash into the larger can or pull the bag out, put a new bag in and put the lid back on the trash can. Then, the child is instructed to carry the trash outside. They are to lift the lid, put the trash in the can, and replace the lid on the outside trash can. It is only then that they have been fully "trained" in the glories of the trash regimen.

Subsequent to the training, the purposeful parent will give their child a clear expectation, such as "I expect you to take out the trash, just as I have shown you, and continue to do so by 5PM each day until the Lord returns!." Of course, one might have to show them more than once how to accomplish the task properly. There may be many a weary parent who are thinking, "I do not want to have to do all that." Yes, it is a tedious process, but it is important not to make the mistake of most, which is to not provide proper instruction or clear expectations. The time spent in the early stages of childhood in proper training are the sowing which will produce a blessed future harvest. A parent will reap what is sown, so sow early and consistently.

Once the child has seen what to do, demonstrated by their parent, they know what is expected without excuse. Thus, the responsibility for the task is shifted from the parent to the child.

## Supervision

The next day, a purposeful parent will naturally check a bedroom or two. To supervise is to ensure that the child has actually accomplished the wishes of the parent. If the parent finds that their child has done the job according to expectations (not perfect, rewarding partial completion encourages the child to do even better the next time) give them appropriate praise. Encourage them for a job well done. However, if the child is five or fifteen minutes late, or have apparently forgotten their responsibility, then what? The parent may, at their discretion, provide a little grace period. But if the parent has supervised the job and it has not been done (at all or properly) confrontation of the child is necessary and appropriate. This will be done within the parents' natural style. For example, the parent might say, "Oh, child of my loins, it is five-twenty." He might say, "Good dad, you can tell time." Then you say, "Ya know, I'm amazed. I looked around the house, and to my amazement and dismay, the trash is still in all the cans." Then Bill says, "Oh, I forgot!" That statement by the child puts the all wise parent in a position of great power. The parent may, in their benevolence, decide to be merciful, which is not recommended, at least in the beginning. Instead the parent might exclaim, "Well, go ahead and take out the trash now, but when you are done, come and see me." When they do, the parent with great delight can move on to the next phase of powerful and purposeful parenting.

## Follow-through and Discipline

It is not discipline to yell at the child because he did not take the trash out. All this teaches the child is procrastination. This is what has been taught to most children in the United States. For most children, it is worth the risk to not do the chore. Why is that? Because the chances of their parent following up and making sure that they were responsible, is 50/50 at best.

Most parents, especially in Western nations, would prefer to be armchair parents, hoping foolishly that their children, being practically perfect like themselves, will automatically obey their parents every request, never disappointing their beloved progeny. What utter drivel! Parents must be willing to actively engage their children, requiring responsible behavior, or the parents and society will suffer the future damage. The child in this illustration needs to learn to be responsible, and will in all likelihood benefit from consequences which fit the offense. Unless it was an act of out and out defiance, the best consequence is a natural or logical one (such as another dirty job, or even taking out the neighbors' trash). Logical and natural consequences, and how to apply the principles of their usage, will be covered in great detail in chapter 10.

## Encouragement

To encourage is more powerful than to praise. Children look up to their parents as godlike figures. A word from them is more powerful than an utterance from the most prominent prophet. When a parent tells the child, preferably with appropriate touch as a positive affirmation, how proud they are for their responsible behavior, how blessed they are to have them as their child, it lifts the view of the child above their present perception of self. Much has been said about self-esteem development in children. The focus has often been on how negative behaviors are produced through negative words. This has been taken to an extreme by some parents, where they will not even tell their child "no!" for inappropriate or wrong behavior. Children need to know their limits. However, when children do things correctly, they need to hear about it, with words of encouragement and affirmation. Statements such as, " I appreciate the good job you did...that was a good job...you are really doing well at following my instructions, that shows you are learning responsibility which pleases me, your mom and the Lord", etc. are life giving to the child. Words of a positive nature go a long way towards encouraging positive behavior. Further, these affirmative words will lift their image of self as a young man or woman of God. Ultimately, what is desired is to bring to the child the understanding that obedience in the small things will produce healthy results for themselves in the future, and will be pleasing to the Lord.

## A Second Goal or Purpose

The primary goal in parenting is to assist ones children in the maturation process. Maturation is in part a process of teaching conformity to commonly held rules and beliefs. Parents do not want their children conformed to a completely secular viewpoint. Ultimately, children are to be transformed into the image of Christ.

Believers' beliefs are different, or at least they should be, from the rest of society. In other words, Christian parents should be listening to the voice of the Lord, through His word, as well as through practical wisdom as taught within the local church. One's Christian commitment should impact the worldview in such a way as to modify or to transform ones entire life. Christians are in the process of the transformation of their thinking so that they no longer reflect the world's view. The worldview of Western culture is often characterized by an overemphasis on materialism and self-centeredness. Because of the Christians' new belief system, which began when they received Christ and continues as they grow in the Lord, should change the core beliefs, attitudes and expectations about self and others.

Christians should be different from the rest of the world, in thinking and attitude. Christians will continue to have the influence of the old nature fighting against the new self for the entirety of life here on earth. Believers are never fully delivered of the influence of the world until they go home to be with the Lord. But all of God's people should be progressively moving farther away from the world and more toward Christ.

In light of this acknowledged truth, if ones beliefs are different, then, their actions should be different as well. Actions follow beliefs. Behavior follows thought. If a person were to state, "I did not think about it, I just reacted," they are less than truthful. They may not have been aware of their thought processes. They may have acted impulsively or instantaneously. This does not excuse the behavior, nor diminish responsibility for their actions. For instance, one may become angry, because of a perceived threat, or may become upset about something the child says. In this instance, the parent reacts in anger or even rage. This can and unfortunately does happen all too often, even in Christian homes. Though it may feel as an impulsive reaction on behalf of the parent towards the child, there is still thought behind the behavior. These impulsive responses are rooted in the attitudes and internal thought life of the parent. If one's heart/mind is changed, the behavior will ultimately change also. If the heart/mind is not brought into conformity with the word of God, the most aggressive and inappropriate behaviors are possible.

Some spiritual leaders, with the best of intentions, have attempted to change behavior externally with a misguided hope that this will change the heart or beliefs as well. It rarely works. Jesus' focus, in His teaching and healing ministry, was a change of heart, which occurs when one encounters Christ at a deep and personal level.

The work of the Holy Spirit continues to effect change, as one looks into the mirror of God's Word in light of ones learned belief system. What most adults have learned from their family of origin and believe to be true must be evaluated within a balanced understanding of the Word of God. With the hope that, if there is a discrepancy between ones beliefs or past training and the Word of God, the parent will willingly forego previously held beliefs and learned behaviors which may not be truth. The parent must be willing to embrace what is truth, and change as required by the word of God. The truth of the Word must be taken into the depths of the heart. If the parent will do so, out of obedience to the Word of God, eventually, not immediately, their behavior will change. Right behavior will follow right thinking.

The reader may be asking, "What does this have to do with Parenting on Purpose?" Everything. Believing parents must have beliefs and actions, which are consistent with a Christian lifestyle. Christians are to be known by their good fruit. Many Christians toot their horn about their beliefs but the proof is in their daily lifestyle, especially at home. The most difficult place to have a consistent life as a Christian is in the crucible of ones home. The world is a piece of cake. The most difficult place to exhibit love, grace, mercy, kindness, forgiveness and honesty is with ones most intimate family. Adolescents are especially gifted at discerning any form of hypocrisy. They tend to exploit this knowledge to their own benefit, not looking in the mirror at their own hypocrisy. They point out their parents' inconsistencies with great delight. Parents often encourage their testimony, empowered by an inconsistent lifestyle. Inconsistent behaviors tend to flow from unrepentance of wrong beliefs manifested in daily behavior.

Wise parents are willing to admit their shortcomings, and make a concerted effort to live their life according to biblical principles. The attitudes of Jesus' life and the apostle's teaching become their goal. Where ones life does not line up, heartfelt repentance is required. Repentance means to change ones thinking, which leads to a change in lifestyle. Where parents find themselves acting in a fashion which is not in the best interests of their child, change is needed and possible. Now that is easy to say, but hard to do. This change of ones behavior begins from the inside, by first admitting it, bringing it to the Lord. To expose ones areas of weakness, bringing it out of darkness and into the light, requires courage and faith. The parent must be willing to confess their sin or weakness. If one is struggling with the process of confession and repentance, find a mature believer to talk with, to help pray through the situation to completion. If one hides sin of any kind, be sure it will eventually be uncovered (Num. 32:23) or manifest in the next generation.

## Forgiveness is an Example

If a parent has offended their child, whether accidentally or on purpose, take a big step, admit it and apologize. The parent will not lose their authority. God gives parental authority. The parent has the authority because of the mere fact of being a parent. Inherent in the office is the authority. God has essentially said, "You are the parent, they are the child." End of discussion. The parent has the authority; it need not be proven, only exercised judiciously and with wisdom. What parents do need to demonstrate is that their life is different, worthy of emulation. It is easier to convince ones children to follow them and the Lord when the parent has the ability to ask for forgiveness when needed.

*"Trust in the Lord with all your heart, lean not on your own understanding, in all your ways acknowledge him and he will direct thy path."*

**Proverbs 3:5-6**

# Chapter 6

# Development: Key to the Child's Kingdom

There are some vital keys found in natural observation to effective training and teaching. The more a parent knows about how children mature, the better able the parent will be to minister to their needs effectively. Please remember that perfect parents do not exist, but excellent ones do. Knowledge of the development of children and God's Word will help even a tentative parent to become the excellent parents God has intended them to be.

### Viva la Difference

All children are similar but there are no two alike. Even identical twins are not actually identical. For example, I was on a plane coming back from Texas and happened to be sitting next to a gentleman who was also part of a ministry. His was with a Lutheran Renewal ministry. After social politeness, he began sharing about his ministry. I happily reciprocated. He began to share in detail about his prayer life. He shared how he was into making a list of the things that he was praying for and that he was really praying and believing God for great things. He further testified of many tremendous miracles through his personal prayer life.

He then shared with me a couple of things so that I could also pray with him. He mentioned that he had twin sons, one of which a few weeks before came out of the closet, telling his mom and dad that he had AIDS. The story the young man told was that he transmitted the disease from a casual sexual encounter with a girl he used to date. The reality is that he had been in the homosexual lifestyle for a number of years and was afraid to tell his parents. He has an identical twin who was as heterosexual as they come. They are identical but they are definitely not the same, even though raised in the same environment. They went in different directions to express their individuality. It was not genetic, but a chosen lifestyle. Many would wonder what went wrong with this family to cause such a problem. Certainly, this man did. One may never fully know why ones children make decisions. It is important to understand there are always differences in children, but there are also many significant similarities, which can be seen during specific developmental time periods.

These similarities have been wonderfully documented through the research of many behavioral scientists, through the discipline known as child development or developmental psychology. Perhaps the most useful and comprehensive developmental approach was developed through the work of Erik Erickson. His work, with minor supplementation from additional sources, is presented here to increase the parents understanding of their individual child. (For more, see Dr. Joseph Bohac's book, *Human Development.*)

All children start the same way, through the miracle of conception. It has been clearly documented that even in the uterus, children feel and perceive sensations. It is amazing how many people can trace their feelings of abandonment or rejection to the reality that the parents did not want the child. They can't see it, they do not remember it, cognitively, but they sense it, they feel it. Even when the parents later embrace the child, recognizing that the baby is beautiful anyway, no matter how this process started, still the child can carry an awesome sense of rejection and abandonment. So beginning from conception, what happens to the child can effect their future development.

Each child has a certain temperament style, a certain way that they approach the world by nature. At the same time the environment children are reared in does impact, shape and mold character and personality. To help understand the various similarities and differences found in children, one must observe child development, starting with infancy through young adulthood. In each stage there is a task that must be accomplished. In other words, every human being has many important things that must be learned. The things that need to be learned are vital for a child to build upon for the next stage of development. No one has ever had absolute perfect development. That is why all people need a Savior. However, an understanding of these stages can help one to parent effectively and avoid mistakes that can cause damage for the next generation.

## Infancy
## Trust vs Mistrust

If you have a child that is in this age group the major task that they need to accomplish is to learn to trust. The child must develop a sense of trust in their caregivers and the environment in key areas. In the physical realm, they are learning the process of eating, sleeping, keeping warm, eliminating and being cleaned up. All those things are very, very important. Most children receive positive care if they grow up in a normal family. There have been numerous studies conducted with children who were raised in orphanages who did not receive anything more than just physical care. Many would die at a very young age because they were not properly stimulated or nurtured. Man does not live on bread alone!

Another area of learning for an infant occurs sensually. This means that infants learn through the process of feeling, of familiarity with the environment. A feeling of well being must be established. Children can sense if they are wanted or if they are not. They sense if they are loved or not. They learn this through the holding, nurturing, caring process from primary caregivers. It is not just food, clothing and shelter. They must be loved. If they are kissed, hugged, stroked, talked to, they will sense that they are in a safe environment versus an unsafe environment.

Primary relationships are very important. Children must develop a trust in the maternal relationship first, then the paternal. Maternal, meaning mom, paternal meaning dad. Dad is important in that process but mom is primary. One of the reasons for that is the breast. Dads do not produce milk, moms do. Thus, there is a natural aspect to mother that father will never be able to provide. This is one of the reasons why moms are most important in the initial stage. They can give to the child what father's cannot give. If you are bottle-feeding, in that case parents are almost equally important. Although mom's instinctually are able to provide a certain amount of nurturing that dad's are clueless about, so usually it is very, very important that you have mom and dad, but mom first.

Children in this stage also need to have continuity and consistency. What I mean by continuity is that the level of care and the type of care is consistent, day after day after day. Not that the child gets changed sometimes and other times you let them cry in their playpen. What that can create is insecurity or mistrust. Many parents were taught that if their children cry, leave them in their crib and they will get over it. This depends upon what they are crying for. Many people will say that moms can tell the difference in the baby's cry. This is not always true. If a child is crying, they are crying for a reason. They are not just exercising their lungs like some doctors have tried to teach. When they cry, it is because they are trying to say something that they obviously cannot say with words, I need, I want. You are not going to spoil them rotten at this age if you pick up and comfort your child.

Children can shape your behavior. I'm sure you know that. You smile at a child, the child smiles back. When they see that their smile creates mom's smile and this gives them more attention, they learn to smile more. This is based upon simple laws of reinforcement. Neither the child nor the parent is being spoiled. Physical discipline of a child during this age is ineffective. You virtually have to catch the child in the act at the time they are doing something wrong or they do not even know what you are talking about or why you are disciplining them. They have an attention span of somewhere between 3 and 5 seconds at age one. Prior to that, it is even less. If a child is reaching out to touch the TV and you have told him no and before you get to him, he grabs his nose (or something else), and you smack him, he will think, "what, I'm not supposed to touch my nose?" They have no concept of being able to link the TV with the discipline. You have to catch them literally right in the act and then usually a slap on the hand is only designed to get their attention, not to hurt them. What they need during this developmental stage is a lot of attention, a lot of nurturing, and a lot of care.

You want them to develop a sense of trust. If they trust, they grow. Prov. 3:5-6 says, *"Trust in the Lord with all your heart, lean not on your own understanding, in all your ways acknowledge him and he will direct thy path."*

What if I do something wrong? Is God going to smack me? How many of us would have been smacked into oblivion by now? All of us. Especially during the time when we are developing a basic sense of trust in God, which is the first few weeks and months of our Christian walk. We do not need to be smacked by a pastor or anyone else.

As a responsible parent, you are responsible for creating an environment that is as safe and nurturing as possible. As parents we are not to yell or scream at a little child. They neither understand nor can handle such treatment. They only learn that they are bad. That is all they can incorporate. Their internal perception becomes, I must be bad, that is why mom or dad is yelling at me. Insecurity and mistrust in relationships will likely occur if there are numerous inconsistencies. Inconsistency, punishment or abandonment can be unfortunate aspects of life. As much as lies within us as parents we are to create an environment of safety.

If a mom falls ill and has to go to the hospital and if baby does not have anyone close to care for him or her, tremendous anxiety for the child may be the result. There may be little one can do about this type of situation. Like so much of life, this anxiety ridden situation becomes something the child will eventually have to overcome. Assisting the child to overcome becomes a primary responsibility of the parent. But for the most part, if children receive consistent care in feeding them, general hygiene, nurturing, including them (such as taking them with us were we go) and being a loving parent, the child will develop a sense of basic trust. Trust is essential for spiritual, emotional and physical development of the child.

## Terrible Two's
## Autonomy vs Shame and Doubt

The ages two to four is the developmental stage called Autonomy versus Shame and Doubt. During this time of the child's life, he or she begins to explore the environment. Hopefully, they are allowed to do so without overbearing restraint. This stage is known as every parent's nightmare, aptly called the terrible two's. During this stage the child expresses autonomy, having to do with the freedom to monitor oneself. They are able to explore their environment. As children reach eighteen months, but with greater gusto at around two years of age, they begin their quest to explore everything. They want to climb on counters and tables; they want to see the blissful results of jumping on or off of something, just because it is there. This often problematic though, rarely fatal behavior is done, not because they are bad children, they are doing this because they can! It is what curious and energetic children do.

One essential as parents is to safe proof the home. A parental responsibility, whether in ones own home or at a friends (or even in-laws!) is to provide a safe environment so they can explore their world with autonomy, and within clear and safe limits. For example, they can explore the whole backyard as long as there is a fence there, that no dog can assault them, and that the grounds are free of highly harmful things. This requires some work on the part of the parent, to insure adequate safety, but it is worth the time. Also, in this stage, the child has to learn what is expected of him, what they can and cannot do. A purposeful parent is beginning the process of setting boundaries and limits on their freedom to explore. Boundaries must be put on their activities to develop self-control.

This is also potty training time. Potty training is primarily an issue of muscle control in terms of the bowel movement. It is also an area of emotional or psychological control. The child wants to control everything. This is why they often use the word "NO!" The reason the two and three year olds say no is because no is easier to say than yes. They can't form the word yes as easily as no, and also they can say no and no feels good. No is a statement of I do not want to, but it does not mean I will not. I am going to say no because I want to say no. "Do you want some ice cream?" They say, "No" as they take the bowl and start to eat. Parents should learn not to take all of this personally. It is easy to personalize the child's no. Yelling, "Do not you say no to me!" rarely modifies the behavior; time will. Yet, regardless of how many times ones precious child might emphatically state no, the parent has a primary task of assisting the child to set boundaries on their activities, to help them develop self-control.

A primary reason to begin to potty train the child, a most important task, is to assist them in learning self-control. Many parents ask, "When is the best time to start training my child?" Training should begin when the child begins to show an interest in having control. If you start a child too young it won't work. Thus, most parents understand that you start by taking the child in to the bathroom and show them the little potty until they start showing an interest in it. You do not force them onto the potty-chair. Why? They are better at being stubborn than you are! It is their time for being anal-retentive (holding on even if it hurts) and anal expulsive (I can go anywhere, anytime!). They will grunt but they will not go. Not for you. Do not set yourself up that way. The child has to show readiness for anything including education. They need to be made aware of your desire for them to accomplish this task, which they will, and at the same time, recognize that they are dealing with issues of control that go beyond just the potty chair.

If a parent tries to over control a child, the child can develop a sense of shame or self-doubt. The child will internalize, "I do not think I can do things on my own. I can only do what my parents say that I can do." Now they obviously would not articulate that; this becomes an internalized belief system. The other side is that if they are allowed to do whatever they want, they develop a sense of omnipotence. There is nothing worse than a child that thinks that they know, can say, and do anything their heart desires. Reality will eventually catch up with the most illusive of self-absorbed people. None of us knows everything or can do everything; only God is omniscient and omnipotent.

The child desires to control everything in their environment. They can not keep their hands off things. From their limited worldview, everything belongs to them. Usually the child continues to need and demand acceptance during this stage. What is meant by acceptance is to accept them, mistakes and all. This does not indicate a tolerance for one who is morally wrong. In truth, a two to four year old child cannot do something morally wrong, in as much as they are not old enough to know what morals are. They have no clear conscience or sense of guilt, lacking the ability to discern right from wrong, unless imposed upon them by adults.

A parent's focus of loving discipline during this stage of development is to begin to teach appropriate versus inappropriate behavior, based upon their age. Instead of right and wrong, should and shouldn't, it is either judicious (it is going to be helpful for the growth of the child) or it is not. If the behavior of the child is not helpful or healthful, it needs to be corrected. Positive parents can correct the majority of inappropriate behavior in a child by simply changing a child's direction. If they are climbing on something, take them down. The parent can put a barrier up so they can't climb and hurt themselves. Many parents are unwilling to inconvenience themselves for the sake of safety. They want to leave all their nice china out, keep all their nick-knacks on the coffee table and attempt to force their child to control their behavior, long before they are old enough to do so. If one leaves a two to four year old child in a room by themselves for fifteen minutes, and then return, the room will no doubt be messy. It is nothing personal. That is what unsupervised children do; and they do it exceedingly well.

Also, most children have a need to control others. They especially want to control mom. Their internalized belief is that "Mom is all mine, Dad is all mine, everything is mine"! Obvious to most parents is the reality that the child's desire and judgment is not to be taken seriously. You can't give them everything that they want. Giving a 4-year-old the keys to the car would not be appropriate. Nor can one give them cookies every time they bark for it. Learning to handle and correct some of the more annoying, attention-seeking behavior is the art of parenting. Remember, if the child is excessively shamed, it can damage their self-image. This is to be avoided to the best of ones ability. The world we live in is highly shame based. Much shaming occurs during the earliest stages of life, when parents in frustration shame their children by placing too high expectations on them or ridicule them when they fail.

Parents who tend to be immature or impulsive themselves can be easily frustrated and have difficulty in controlling their own emotions. They may feel as though their world is out of control. Then the child, who is also looking for control, and the parent's needs collide. This creates an all too real and often painful conflict. This is classically referred to as a power struggle. Truly, from outside observation, most power struggles appear as quite silly. Here's a three-year-old child who's running mom and dad around like they have a ring in their nose, manipulating them at every turn. The parents remain in a constant state of anxiety, frustrated because they do not know what to do with their child. They know they must discipline them, control them, at least do something! But they have a learned helplessness, with barely a clue as to what to do. In frustration they can even do the unthinkable, and abuse and/or neglect their child. Tragically, this happens more often than one cares to know, including in Christian homes. However, if the child is insufficiently disciplined, they will develop a sense of omnipotence, becoming increasingly unmanageable.

Another difficulty for parents is the fact the child can become quite secretive. That is normal. Children want to keep their own counsel. They like to hide things from mom and dad. The things hidden are rarely bad things, they are just things. Why do they do things in secret? They do so because of the developmental need of the child. They are essentially stating by their secretive behavior, "I want to develop my own space, my own autonomy." Wise parents learn to give their child some room to breathe. Providing ample opportunity to develop some of their own world is quite healthy and growth producing.

Also, it is helpful to remember that young children will not share well. In fact, they do not want to share with anyone, unless it is to their advantage. And why is this? This occurs because they are two to four years of age. It is normal. They are not lying, cheating, or stealing. In fact, a child at this age does not steal, they simply take something. Sometimes they take things that do not belong to them. If they can, they will. It is nothing personal. In their mind, the item of desire was in the line of sight, so they took it. Their taking gives the parent an opportunity to bring loving correction to their behavior. Not done in anger, but with firm love.

A parents' purpose is to bend the child's will, not break it. One of the finest books written on this subject is *Dare to Discipline* by Dr. James Dobson. He presents some of the clearest and most comprehensive information on how to bend but not break a child's will. A parent must allow their child the freedom to make some of their own decisions or they will develop an inadequate ability to make strong decisions when they really need to. Their sense of will can be impaired. Saying no is a great skill children need to develop. It will help them, especially when they encounter a used car salesman in later life!

This stage is also characterized by what's called parallel play. Picture two children at this age (two to four years) in a sandbox. It may look like the children are playing together but they are not. They are playing parallel to each other. Sometimes if they get along fairly well, they will switch toys. I'll take yours and you can have mine. It looks as though they are sharing, but they are not. I'm taking, you're taking. We are playing along side of each other. This is a lot like many couples in marriage. Getting couples to do things together sometimes is almost impossible because they are stuck, in terms of their emotional development, at this early stage. They do not know how to initiate relationships. Instead they use shame or create doubt in the relationship in order to gain control of their spouse, rather than more appropriately loving their spouse.

## Pre-school Stage
## Initiative vs Guilt

The preschool stage is four to six years of age. It is called Initiative versus Guilt. This is a time that children want to do things on their own without constant supervision. They are trying to master their environment. They are beginning to sense responsibility for the self, mentally and physically. They want to demonstrate the ability to initiate acts of freedom or greater autonomy. For instance, they are going to want to go play next door with their friend all by themselves. They want to be able to move a little farther away from mom and dad and take a little more responsibility for themselves. They begin to attempt to achieve certain goals. They are usually very short-lived goals but they are goals none the less. They try to accomplish some kind of task on their own, yet with a continued focus on pleasing mom and dad.

Guilt comes from the over-development of too much initiative being shown. In other words, if they do too many things that aren't properly rewarded or positively rewarded, they can develop a sense of guilt. The virtue to be achieved in this stage is finding a purpose for living. Thus, they are learning to take initiative, which moves them towards finding a reason to be a part of the family system. They are looking to be productive and to fit in the larger circle. To be is to do.

Four to six-year-olds are still in a pre-learning stage. Some children at this age are ready to learn. They are able to read, do mathematics, etc. Some children will not be ready until seven or even eight years of age. That is why the decision of when to start a child in school is very important. Most school districts give readiness tests to determine whether or not a child is ready to learn developmentally. If they are not and you push them into school because they are five years of age, their learning can be hampered. You will be setting the child up for guilt and failure. Many times they will carry this sense of failure throughout their entire lives. The decision about school is a very important one that must be prayerfully made during this stage. (However, please note that 95% of children are ready by age 5).

## Ages Six Through Twelve
## Industry vs Inferiority

Then comes late childhood, ages six through twelve. The primary developmental task to be mastered is Industry versus Inferiority. The child having mastered (at least fairly well we hope) control of their bowels, attempts to take control of their own imagination or thought life. Until approximately age six, children spend from 75% to 95% of their day in a world of their own, inside their own head. Children have a highly elaborate and rich life of fantasy. From simple outside observation it may appear that they are in the real world, but they do not think in a concrete or logical fashion. This gives reason to the child's ability to play games such as cowboys and Indians, changing roles at whim, living and dying, only to do it again and again. None of the play means more than fun, because none of it is real. It is all fantasy. This is a protective mechanism that helps in early survival.

Beginning around age six to seven, and continuing through about age twelve, children learn to take control of their imagination. The ability to concentrate gradually increases, as does the ability to stay on task. This ability is of great importance in an educational setting, as the ability to concentrate and stay on task is vital for educational success. Children with a limited or delayed ability to do so often suffer from ADD, or Attention Deficit Disorder. They are unable to stay on task and master their own ability to concentrate, and require special education to assist them in their emotional and educational growth.

During this stage, a child's' desire is to accomplish things and/or show forms of industry. They thrive on being productive. Children have a deep need to please mom and dad, and this desire is extended to the teacher. In fact, many times children will fall in love with their teacher. They do so because the teacher provides them with very positive reinforcement for their ability to produce, which fills an emotional developmental need. Diligence is what they are working towards, which means to work towards rewards which are accomplishable.

Further, a sense of vision begins to emerge during this stage. That is, they begin to see themselves into the future. Moment by moment living gives way to week by week. The possibility of the continuation of life beyond the day becomes a reality. This becomes a strategic time for children to come to know the Lord. It is natural for them to ask questions about God and the future. They have the ability to think in terms of life and death; death as being permanent rather than transitory state. Thus, they are able to understand the need for heaven and the need for a savior.

At all times, they are preparing themselves for the adult world. Purposeful parents assist their children in the creation of a sense of adequacy rather than inferiority, which is a feeling of not being good enough compared to parents, peers, etc. By far, parents have the greatest influence. Parents can significantly assist their children by reinforcing the productivity of their children, or their ability to do things well in their own areas of giftedness. Unfortunately, many parents attempt to vicariously live out their childhood through their child. Parents who force a child into piano, athletics or various other activities in order to fulfill the parents' desires do so to the detriment of the children. A classic example of this is the Little League parent, where dad is rooting, screaming and criticizing if the child does not perform to the parents' expectation. The child responds by constantly trying harder to perform so that dad (or mom) will be pleased.

By age twelve, if a child has not achieved a sense of belonging through their industry they may develop a sense of inferiority or discouragement. Finding a place in the family, and a belief that they are good enough is a core component of a healthy self-worth. Discouraged children may give up the will to try, limiting their ability to reach necessary milestones. A sense of failure in a child can set the child up for a very rocky adolescence.

During pre-adolescence, children tend to see the world through a black and white mentality. There are either good people or bad people, with no gray areas of thought. Sometimes they can shift back and forth. Everything is quite concrete in their thinking. Pre-adolescents are rarely able to show mercy. If someone that has done something wrong they are all bad, and if they have done something good, they are all good. They can't be both. Often they believe that good things happen to good people and bad things happen to bad people.

This black and white belief system is similar to that of ancient Judaism. They espoused a theological belief that if a person prospered it was because they were good and because God was blessing them. If a person did not prosper, it meant that God was angry and they were bad. If things went wrong, it must be due to secret sin, (i.e. see the book of Job). Unfortunately, there are many in the church today that believe in a similar manner. If a person does not prosper, if they are not deliriously happy, if one is not in perfect health, well then they must be in secret sin. Those that are prospering are more spiritual and favored by the Lord, and those who suffer must have deserved their plight. If that were really true, then God especially loves the Japanese, because they are financially prospering and are a blessed people. This type of thinking does not fit with a Christian adult. The rain falls on the just and the unjust alike. Young children cannot understand the often-harsh realities of life. They are not supposed to be able to understand. They will learn more of the inconsistencies of life as they mature.

If abuse occurs at this age, the child will experience intense guilt. As stated above, their perception is that bad things happen to bad people. Thus, they must be bad. It is in this age (anywhere from six to twelve), that the highest level of child abuse, particularly sexual abuse, occurs. From six to twelve, many anxiety-based disorders, fears and depression, caused by abuse can occur. A further result of abuse may include the incorporation of negative beliefs of self, an inferiority attitude, and tormenting memories that can arrest normal development.

The virtue to be achieved in this stage is personal competence. In other words, if a child learns that they can do, are competent to accomplish, this skill carries the child with a sense of confidence and competence throughout their life. Unfortunately, many people, even in the church, have little sense of competence. Pastors bemoan the difficulty of motivating God's people to works of service. It is often like pulling teeth with a hammer to move a Christian to action. They just can't. Most of their lack of confidence can be traced to problems during this developmental stage. This will become clearer when related to adult life, to be explored in a later section of this book.

## Adolescence
### Identity Development vs Role Confusion

Prior to adolescence, and in the early middle school years, the educational system becomes increasingly more difficult. Social pressures intensify. If the emerging young adult does not feel connected to their family, with their church or a positive peer group, they begin to look for substitutes, other groups which may satisfy their need to belong, be appreciated, and cared for. Many a parent has wondered "What happened to my child? At thirteen they just went bananas. I do not know what happened to my little girl (boy)."

The behavior and personality of an adolescent is made up of many factors. One primary dynamic is the strength of development that undergirds the child from his family of origin. Adolescents who have extreme difficulty (a small percentage), generally have a history of limited encouragement, a chaotic family upbringing, and personal deficits. Encouragement or the lack thereof is one key component in good children having hard times in their teenage years. For example, if a child comes home with a 'D' on their report card, it is acknowledged that the 'D' is not a good grade. It is not the end of the world either. The significance of a single grade (or for that matter, a single chore being done right on time, etc.) depends on the circumstances surrounding he low grade. If the has done their best, and they have not performed to expectation, grace and mercy needs to be applied.

### From Down Under

I was in Australia when I received a phone call from Rebecca, my eldest daughter. She was in ninth grade and was having great difficulty with Algebra. Her call was to inform me that she had completed her class, and received a "D" in Algebra. When I was in school, I received a D- in Algebra (also in ninth grade). In truth, I deserved an F. But as the instructor told me, "Your next year's teacher does not deserve someone as stupid as you are, so I am going to pass you." I was so happy; I just wanted out! Therefore, I had such sympathy for my precious daughter Rebecca. She had struggled all year long with her Algebra. She did her homework. She even had a tutor. Unfortunately, she inherited my brain cells or lack thereof. So as she related to me her news, we began to laugh. The laughter was from relief that the course was over and joy at her success. I knew that she had tried her best and as far as I was concerned, she conquered the demon! Meaning she survived!

If the parental attitude is such that a grade, or the style of hair, becomes an "Oh my God! You have not performed to my expectations!" it can squelch the child's normal desire to take initiative. Then, when adolescence arrives, and the child has the energy and intelligence to question parental expectations, conflict beyond the norm can easily develop.

## On To Adolescence

Adolescence is not a disease but it does seem like it. It is a time of identity development, or the solidification of ones perception of who they are and their place in the world. During this phase, the internal question of the adolescent is, "Who am I and how do I fit into society?" It is the development of a stable understanding of self that they seek. The adolescent knows that there is a defined role to play in life that is unique to them. The discovery of their role is the task of adolescence, and the role of a parent must shift to accommodate the adolescents need. Teenagers require coaching and guidance rather than parental dictates appropriate to an early stage of development.

One of the difficulties in learning what one's identity is includes the adolescent tendency towards being very self-conscious and easily embarrassed. Most teenagers are socially awkward, unsure of their strengths and weaknesses, struggling with their peer and adult acceptability, unsure whether they are liked or disliked. This instability in the adolescent is easily seen but generally misunderstood or over reacted too by adults and peers alike. Thus, it takes wisdom and flexibility to assist the adolescent to transition this important phase of their young life.

When an adolescent freaks out (for instance, because they have a pimple on date night!), it is because their whole life is weighing in the balance. To most parents, who are thankfully light years away from their last pimple crisis, it is only a pimple, it will be gone in three days. THREE DAYS! To the teen, that is an eternity! The adolescent, lacking a solidified identity, (that says, if someone is going to like me or not like me because I have a pimple, who cares), this is a major concern. They actually believe that what their peers think about them is life and death. Since they are most self-conscious, unsure of their identity, they need understanding and support. Further complicating normal adolescent stability is the awakening sexual desires. These desires, which are intense but imminently controllable, need to be understood and proper teaching as to Gods' plan and purpose for sexuality must be clearly and openly presented. They need to know who they are, not merely in terms of heterosexual or homosexual. That is pretty easy to see. They need only look in the mirror. But what does their maleness or femaleness mean in terms of relationships, and as it relates to the word of God. Further, their masculinity or their femininity must be affirmed, reinforced by the same and opposite sex parent.

The father is the primary reinforcer of both positive male and female identity. Research has shown that the absence of a father or poor fathering produces a foundation of identity confusion. Emotional affirmation is a primary function of the father. It is inherent in the male species to reinforce sexual identity, both for the adolescent male and female. When the daughter comes downstairs in a dress, looking most lovely, the father has the opportunity to affirm the daughters' femininity. If dad sits on the coach, and ignores the daughter when she asks how she looks, the fathers' wife should hit him with a frying pan! He has certainly earned it. The appropriate response to a daughter would be, "Wow, you look marvelous!" An appropriate and positive response reinforces in the daughter a belief that she is attractive as a female. That is very important. Mom can say she looks pretty, but it does not carry the same weight of impact. A mother is wonderful, necessary and always loved, but moms are supposed to love, give compliments, etc. But when dad notices his budding beauty and comments appropriately, it begins to transform the child into a woman.

Just as femininity is reinforced by the affirmation of the father, the father reinforces masculinity. For some reason, moms do not have the gift to reinforce masculinity. It is assumed that mothers will love and nurture their children. Fathers inherently carry an authority and mystery that imprints at a deep level a sense of worth if positive affirmation is given to their children.

For young men, if mom says, "You look very handsome or muscular today," the young man may feel complemented yet, "What does she know?" However, when dad grabs the boys arm, squeezes the muscle and comments positively, it reinforces the masculinity within the boy. Not only can and should strength and power be reinforced, but also the masculine image of self-control, kindness, love and gentleness, generosity and all of the other qualifications found in the Fruit of the Spirit as described in the Word of God. These attributes are also a part of masculinity. Quality time between the father and child can reinforce the beauty and uniqueness of each child, as well as the characteristics of God to be manifested.

During adolescence, identity confusion (not knowing who one is or how they fit in the world) can result in many symptoms of concern. They include a sense of isolation, a lack of comfort with limited peace, emptiness and anxiety, with much difficulty in making decisions. Often anger and rebellion towards society, parents being the chief proponents of what society is, can result. Certainly, not all children will respond to adolescence with negativity, but most every teenager will do some responding and adjusting. The reason for this is multiple. There are specific hormones being secreted into their system that brings significant changes of mind and body. Some days when your daughter says, "If you touch me I will kill you!" it does not really mean much. It just means she's having a bad hair day. Parents need not become overwrought by little things.

The virtue to be achieved in this stage is fidelity. Solidifying a positive value structure and caring for others is essential. In other words, if the adolescent will learn fidelity or faithfulness in relationships during the adolescent period, this will set the stage for positive decision making in terms of marriage and family life. Each relationship prepares them for future vocational decisions, and especially the decision of when and to whom they will marry. Parents will want their adolescent to learn to be faithful and to complete things that they commit to. If the adolescent begins something one day, works on it for two or three days and then quits, they may learn habits of failure rather than success. Eventually, adolescents must learn to stick with a task until completion, keeping their commitments, which builds faithfulness or fidelity, a necessary trait for successful adult transition.

My wife and I looked forward to our girls reaching adolescent years. They were able to carry on a coherent conversation. Parents do not have to dress and act like teenagers to relate to teenagers. The parents would look like fools if they tried. But a parent does need to spend enough time with their teen to know their hearts, what is important in their lives. If a parent will make the investment they can have a truly excellent relationship with their adolescent.

Erickson and other writers have advanced many other developmental scenarios, but for parenting on purpose those presented here are sufficient. The reader is encouraged to study more on this important topic. One of the best books available today on human development is Dr. Joseph J. Bohac's book, **_Human Development - A Christian Perspective_** which expands this teaching on developmental stages, and their importance in understanding children, and God's creation in general. It is highly recommended reading.

*"Do unto others as you would have them do unto you."*

**Matthew 7:12**

# Chapter 7

# Environmental Impact

The personality and temperament of a child can range from passive to aggressive, dependent to independent. Every child is unique. However, the majority of children carry certain traits in common. These include a need for love, discipline, and freedom. Developmental needs of the child must be met according to the time and season.

The question to be addressed in this chapter is, "What is child training and how does one mold or shape a child in a purposeful direction?" There are specific strategies for training, discipline and teaching that have their basis in principles of human behavior. These strategies, which a parent can apply to their child, will help a parent to remain relatively sane and functional as a parent.

Child training, by definition, is the means by which a parent or other caregiver lovingly assists the child through self-discovery, guidance, encouragement and by example, to develop the potential of their total personality. In the Constitution of the United States it states that "All men are created equal." That is true in the eyes of God but not everybody is equal. Some people have greater giftings and abilities than others. Even the Bible concurs with this truth. Jesus taught in Matthew 25:14-30 that there are different talents for different individuals. Jesus had an expectation that all His disciples would be faithful stewards of the gifts given by the Lord. A major mistake frequently made by the most loving of parents is in comparing themselves with their child or other children with their child. Essentially, such comparisons are totally irrelevant. All children are unique, having an innate ability from God. The responsibility of a parent is to determine with God's help what that potential is. If vocational potential of a child is to faithfully work for the rest of their lives in a blue-collar job, then help them to achieve their potential. To attempt to force them to become a rocket scientist will only frustrate both child and parent. It is fruitless to attempt to vicariously live life through one's children.

A parents' best hope is to draw out of their children the potential of their personality, to help them become responsible and mature human beings. This is why in most societies, parents are held legally liable and morally responsible for their children, up until age eighteen. If a parent were to allow their child, even at seventeen plus years of age, illegal or damaging, they could end up paying the bills. As parents, responsibility can be shared but not neglected until the child is of legally age. A parent's goal is to assist the adolescent to become mature enough to handle adult decisions, long before they actually need to.

## Delightful Discipline

In child discipline, the purpose is to clearly establish guidelines of expected behavior. In order to properly discipline, one must first provide clearly established guidelines of expected behavior. Of course, the age of the child will determine the level of explanation of the expected behavior. For instance, with a 1-year-old child, a simple command is the most beneficial, because they cannot understand a parent's instruction. Expectations can be presented to a child by example, by what the parent allows and disallows. Providing healthy models for the child to follow is the best form of training.

Over many years of counseling, I have had the delight and chagrin of observing hundreds of well-intentioned parents. One common scenario of difficulty surrounds the feeding of a toddler. The child is in their high chair and the parents allow their child to slop food in any direction. They barely notice the food flying, or the concern of others in the same room. Other parents, more strict and meticulous, will pull the plate away and give it back, over and over again, attempting to win the battle of the food fight. There is probably some balance between the two parenting styles that can be gained. Balance comes when the parent keeps in focus the goal of the parenting of young children, which is to train them in functional behaviors (how to eat properly, social graces, etc.). One has to judge how important a specific behavior is in the long haul of child rearing. Is a mess today that high of a priority that the parent might want to withhold food for a while until the child is more ready to eat? In some cases yes, in some no. If a parent does pull the plate away, the child will soon learn what is expected from them. They may slop it all over their face, but a least it won't end up on the ceiling.

Purposeful parents develop guidelines to bring control and correction of negative behavior. Negative is defined as not being beneficial to the child or society. I have seen parents watch their children hit another child and say and do nothing about it. The response to violence, if it is a two-year-old punching a two-year-old, is not to punch the perpetrating two-year-old. That would be child abuse. However, a responsible parent will correct this behavior by physically withdrawing the child from the situation and telling them that their behavior is inappropriate. It is not ok for a child to hit another, excepting in self-defense.

If their child hit first, it is hoped that the other child's parents are reinforcing the same thought that violence is inappropriate. It is often impossible to determine who hit whom first. Unless the event was personally observed, one cannot sit in judgment. Of course, the natural inclination will be to protect <u>one's own</u> child. However, parents need to support each other where possible and reinforce that this type of negative behavior is unacceptable. Correct behavior by stopping it in the most loving way possible and the least restrictive manner that one can. This should be done without shaming or debasing the child in the process.

Here is presented some general guidelines which can help a parent in their decision making process.

1. Obedience to the word of God and submission to legitimate authority is to be modeled by parents and developed in children. For example, I remember as a child hearing my mother exclaim, "What would Jesus do?" Of course, I had no idea what Jesus thought (I was not even fully aware of who Jesus was!). My mother's intent was to use the highest authority available to assist her in the parenting role. I am not suggesting that using Jesus for support is the most effective, but depending upon the age of the child, a parent will want to instruct their child in Biblical principles at a level of understanding that leads to personal application. It is unnecessary to teach bible principles with a prophetic, "Thus saith the Lord." It is not terribly impressive to children. However, teaching the principles of fairness, justice, forgiveness, mercy, kindness, and love will eventually have a positive impact. How many times will it be necessary to teach a child these principles before they become a part of their acted upon character? Probably a few hundred times, maybe more. Teaching and training take time and often-painstaking patience, but eventually positive and consistent sowing <u>will</u> reap a harvest of blessings.

2. Teach children to obey the God-ordained authorities (Teachers, police, pastors). What a joy to observe small children run up exclaiming, "pastor, pastor, pastor", grabbing hold of the pastor's leg, hugging it

with all their might. This expression of pure love and affection towards this recognized personification of father should be freely encouraged in children. However, if a child were to hit the pastor, the reaction by any and all adults in the area should be much different. It does not matter the pastor or his/her reputation. That behavior by the child would be totally inappropriate. The child would benefit from proper discipline for such behavior.

Please remember that the word of God places importance on proper submission to God ordained authority. For instance,

> *"Obey those who rule over you, and be submissive, for they watch out for your souls, as those who must give account. Let them do so with joy and not with grief, for that would be unprofitable for you."*
> (Hebrews 13:17, NKJV)

In this passage of scripture, the writer speaks of the importance of obedience to those in legitimate authority. Further, the Apostle Paul states;

> *"Everyone must submit himself to the governing authorities, for there is no authority except that which God has established. For rulers hold no terror for those who do right, but for those who do wrong. Do you want to be free from fear of the one in authority? Then do what is right and he will commend you. For he is God's servant to do you good. But if you do wrong, be afraid, for he does not bear the sword for nothing, He is God's servant, an agent of wrath to bring punishment on the wrongdoer. Therefore, it is necessary to submit to the authorities, not only because of possible punishment but also because of conscience. This is also why you pay taxes, for the authorities are God's servants, who give their full time to governing. Give everyone what you owe him: If you owe taxes, pay taxes; if revenue, then revenue; if respect, then respect; if honor, then honor. Let no debt remain outstanding, except the continuing debt to love one another, for he who loves his fellowman has fulfilled the law. The commandments, 'Do not commit adultery,' 'Do not murder,' 'Do not steal,' 'Do not covet,' and whatever other commandment there may be, are summed up in this one rule: 'Love your neighbor as yourself.' Love does no harm to its neighbor. Therefore love is the fulfillment of the law."*
> (Romans 13:1-8)

Paul's primary concern for the church in Rome was to learn to be submissive to the Lordship of Christ as demonstrated by proper submission to authority. Authority is "a minister of God to you for good." God has established the authorities that exist. Consequently, a person who rebels against authority is rebelling against what God has instituted, and those who do so will bring judgment on themselves. So much of the rebellious discord seen in young people in the church and society is a direct result of not having learned this vital lesson.

3. Further, parents must teach children to respect the rights of others. This includes the property rights of neighbors and merchants. How do children learn this? They learn respect by example and by correction. If a child observes adults throwing paper out of a window, they will likely follow in kind. If a parent lies on their tax return, cheats on their expense report, or steals small supplies from the office, children notice. A parents' inappropriate behavior makes correcting the child's behavior most difficult. Children are the first to remind parents of their inconsistency. Parents must strive to be positive role models as well as a corrector of the child's misbehavior.

4. Parents must make the family a priority for their children. For example, some families eat dinner at the dinning room table. This activity is seen as a highly valued time of family communication. However, if a family eats dinner together on TV trays, it probably will not destroy them. What to do and how to express one's family life depends upon family goals. It is very difficult to have a good conversation with the TV on. So, if the family goal is to relax, rest, watch TV and enjoy a meal, then set the proper stage according to the preference of the family. If open family communication is the goal, then a more serene forum might be necessary. It is not a violation of God's laws to have the TV on. God desires the family to work together, to accomplish goals together. However, there is much latitude in how to accomplish the task. What parents allow or disallow is often a matter of personal preference.

5. Children should be taught to help one another. This is a wonderful skill to teach through word and deed. One of the reasons that people are so selfish is because they have been socialized to be that way. The prevailing attitude of Western society is to take care of number one. This self-centeredness is quite natural in young children, as their perception of reality is egocentric. A parents' goal is to transition their

children to another and ultimately a Christocentric orientation, serving God and others with gladness of heart.

6. Remember the golden rule. When I was growing up, all parents espoused to their children the golden rule. *"Do unto others as you would have them do unto you."* (Matthew 7:12 & Luke 6:31). Currently this teaching emphasis is out of vogue. Now it is do unto others <u>before</u> they do to you. This prevalent attitude is modeled on virtually every television program. A wise parent will assist their children to learn to observe the golden rule, and demonstrate this type of love in their adult relationships. Children deserve to have the rich heritage of biblically based teaching and training, filled with the love, compassion and loving discipline of Father God.

*"But if any of you lacks wisdom, let him ask of God who gives to all men generously and without reproach. And it will be given to him. But let him ask in faith, without any doubting. For the one who doubts is like the surf of the sea, driven and tossed by the wind. For let not that man expect that he will receive anything from the Lord, being a double minded man, unstable in all his ways."*

**James 1:5**

# Chapter 8

# Understanding Children's Goals

In an earlier section of this book, the various developmental stages were discussed in some detail. One can often tell, in hindsight, where a parent's difficulties were growing up by interacting with ones own, or other children. When a child's behavior triggers certain responses in the parent, it is rarely because of what the child is doing. It is because the parent is identifying something that they are doing with a conflict inside themselves. That is one of the ways to become aware of an area of emphasis needs to be applied in the parenting process. It is a very important concept to understand. If a parent who is observing a child's behavior experiences a specific emotion, such as anger, frustration, or even a desire to act in revenge towards the child, it is usually because the child is doing something that triggers an unresolved conflict from the parent's childhood. If the parent can become aware of their anger or frustration, and act in an opposite fashion, resolution of the parental problem can begin, and avoidance of the perpetuation of the problem to the next generation can be established. It is often characteristics in the child which are not acceptable to the parent, or behaviors which are reminders of wounds from the past are the cause of overreactions in parents. Doing the opposite behavior of what caused a wound in the parent to their child can be healing to the parent and provide preventative medicine to the child. In other words, if it was natural in ones family of origin to have been overly corrected for certain behaviors, and then the parent observes similar behavior in their child, they may overcorrect as well. However, if the parent sees the problematic behavior in the child, but instead of overcorrecting (such as spanking in anger) the parent embraces the child with control and speaks directly to bring about correction (perhaps with time out), the parent will successfully help the child. By correcting the behavior in a more positive and effective manner, the prevention of problems and the process of healing in the parent is begun.

This is one of the wonderful things about being a parent. Parents have a dual opportunity. They can reinforce all the garbage of the past and build on it. In other words, make life worse. Or, they can begin to bring healing into their generation and future generations by acting differently toward problem situations when they arise (which they will). In order to change the patterns of the present and future generations, a parent must be willing to remove the mask of self-deception, becoming aware of ones own feelings and responses towards their children. Rather than simply projecting blame, and placing responsibility on others for wrong or inappropriate actions towards children, parents must be willing to take ownership or responsibility for actions, and thus grow. If a parent practices the projection of blame for parental difficulty and dysfunction, the learned dysfunctional patterns are likely to continue.

## Goals of Misbehavior[5]

All behavior has a reason and purpose to it. Just as one's parenting should have a purpose, to raise children to maturity so that they will be a blessing to the rest of the world, so children's behavior has a goal or a purpose. Understanding the goals of a child's behavior or misbehavior will assist the parent to effectively cope with and even modify negative, problematic behavior. Provided here are the four goals of children's misbehavior and how a parent can use this knowledge for successful parenting.

### Attention

The first goal is that of **attention**. Children need attention and they need to be attended to. The younger the child, the more attention they are going to require. Children naturally require the nurture of parents, which include being attended to, talked to, touched and cared for. When a child does not feel they are receiving enough attention, or if they are very high maintenance children, they have a greater need for attention. Children have an internal belief that they are only worthwhile when receiving attention. Further, through a process of the relationship between the parent and the child, children learn that negative attention is better than no attention at all. If a child is only attended to when doing something wrong, when they are poking and pestering their parent, they will continue that behavior because it is actually being reinforced. How? The parent does give the attention when the child pleads for it. After the explanation of the four goals, some examples of this and the other goals will be presented. Let it suffice to say that attention is one of the primary goals of

---

[5]For more information and advanced training on these concepts see, *Children: The Challenge* by Rudolf Dreikurs and *Systematic Training for Effective Parenting* by Donald Dinkmeyer.

children, and a source of concern and consternation in most parents. When a child is misbehaving and the parental response is irritation and frustration, it is generally an indication that the child is seeking attention from the parents. This attention-seeking behavior may be positive or negative. More on this and the "cure" later.

The number two goal of behavior is **power**. Power equals control for positive parenting purposes. Power needs to be shared between parent and child. The child needs to obtain more power or a little more control over time. In the discussion of child development, the concepts of autonomy, initiative, etc. have been introduced. These important developmental skills need to increase as children grow older. Often a child has a high need for power or control and the parent also has a high need for the same. This can create a very explosive power struggle. Anger may result as an expression of power. Generally, the power or expression of anger will result in the child receiving what they want or the parent what they want. One side will need to retreat because of the anger. If the parent becomes incensed by their child's childish behavior, generally it is because the child is (by their behavior) asking for power which is perceived as threatening to the parent's sense of authority or power.

A third theme or goal of a child's misbehavior can be **revenge**. What a terrible word! Children can express themselves by hurting others in a similar fashion as they feel they have been hurt. Normally a child with revenge as a goal feels, for whatever reason, as though they have been hurt by being neglected, rejected, punished or abandoned. The focus of their revenge is normally directed at parents, though it can be expressed at siblings or friends. Essentially, they are taking out those feelings on others. They feel emotionally hurt or deprived and are attempting to get even. When this is directed at a parent the normal parental response is to feel **hurt**. In counseling parents I will often hear them say, "I do not know why my child does that, they keep hurting me." When one is attacked, it is quite human to want to respond in kind. What most parents will do when they feel they are being hurt is to state internally or externally, "Well, I'll show him and hurt them back." That is of course, how cycles of abuse can begin. If a child's behavior elicits within a parent an internal response of hurt and desires for retaliation, the child's theme is revenge.

The fourth primary goal of misbehavior is a **display of inadequacy**. That is, the child has become completely discouraged in their search to belong. They no longer have expectations of themselves, believing that they are helpless to achieve or belong. This goal does not manifest instantaneously. It happens over an extended period of time. The child will begin to express verbally and behaviorally that nothing they do is good enough. I've counseled with many families that carry this sense of helplessness. It develops from a belief that no matter what they did, it never would be pleasing to the parents. One possible scenario, which could reinforce this belief, is when the child was assigned a task to do, after they had completed it, mom or dad would follow after them and re-do the task. This re-doing of the child's work can strip away some of the child's sense of autonomy, and the ability to take initiative is lessened significantly. This behavior on the part of generally perfectionist parents can lower a positive self-worth and self esteem. Eventually they can become so discouraged they quit, developing a sense of total inadequacy. Essentially, what a parent will experience with a child who has this goal is a feeling of despair. They will state, "I do not know what to do with my child." They will either try to totally rescue the child, doing everything for them so that they do not have to face the criticism of not being adequate, or, they may give up themselves. Essentially, giving up on the child is the last thing the child wants or needs. The child will experience the giving up as abandonment, leaving the child to its own devices.

## Some Sanctified Solutions

Ignorance is *not* bliss! Parents can choose to understand, grow and change. It is possible to develop healthy new patterns for the next generation. To do so, the parent must set their heart to the task. This process begins with a review of family history, continuing with careful monitoring of one's own feelings, then acting strategically based upon these feelings with new, more functional behaviors. Every behavior begins as an attempt to meet a legitimate need. How one feels and thus responds to a child's behavior will provide vital information on what the child's problems, needs and goals are. All parents can learn much about their child based upon how the child responds to parental action.

It is fairly easy to correct short-term problematic behavior. The discipline, which actually ceases negative behavior for a short period of time, is to smack him or her. Their behavior will stop almost immediately. Immediately, that is, until the parent turns their back on the child. Then of course, they will do the negative behavior again and again. Quite likely, the next time the behavior will be worse, and they will have resentment built in on top of it. Corporal punishment works short term. It does not work long term. It is a temporary solution to a (possibly) permanent problem. The desired result of corrective discipline is to train and develop ones child for the future. The best way to respond to the child's misbehavior, after insuring that a legitimate infraction has been made, is to monitor carefully ones own feelings and respond according to the need of the child at the moment. Admiralty, this is easier said than done. However, the doing is very possible, with practice. Thank the Lord He gives us 18+ years to get things right! Let's now look at the goals of misbehavior and the strategic responses to eradicate problem behavior.

## Attention

All children, for that matter, all people need to be attended to by significant others. Thus, before dismissing a child's behavior as simply attention seeking, the question as to the legitimacy of their need must be addressed. Some children seek attention because they are not receiving enough attention in a positive way from their parents. If this is the case, then giving the positive attention is the answer to the problem. The empty cup must be filled. However, if the attention-seeking behavior is not appropriate, then the best strategy is to ignore the child's behavior. Again, this is easy to say, not always easy to do. It is especially difficult to deal with problem behavior if the parent/child interaction is in public. It is in the public arena, such as at a supermarket or in church, where children perform best, seeking attention from mom or dad. Most mothers will attest to the fact that they can never go to the restroom all by themselves. That is, without a child coming in and demanding immediate attention. Or, the phone rings and all Hades breaks loose in the house. Why? Because mom is giving her attention to someone or something else. It seems as though when the parents are available and have the energy to attend to the child, the child lacks interest. That's kids; that's just the way they are.

How can a parent best respond? To begin with, the parent should ignore the behavior, while at the same time looking for opportunities to give attention when the child is doing well. Positive attention should be especially given when the child is not even asking for it. This will provide to the child a sense of their significance, showing that they belong and are important. This is a preventative measure, used to cause a cessation of that behavior. This does not work the first time or every time.

Developmentally, the younger the child, the more they do need attention. When a child is incessantly demanding attention and the parent ignores it, initially the attention seeking behavior will increase. The child hopes that if they try harder their parent will give in. However, if the parent will remain steadfast, and not give in (or give in periodically, which reinforces the behavior even more powerfully) to the demands of the child, the behavior will eventually stop. Of course, ignoring does not always work. At times, the parent must firmly stop the child's behavior by using "time out" and making clear that now is not the time for attention. The goal is to train them to ask for attention at appropriate times and delay gratification. Children that are constantly attended to, beyond the infant stage, will often develop into rather obnoxious children, carrying a self-importance which will be quite detrimental to their growth as people.

## Power

If power is the theme, strategic withdrawal without anger is the first step. Unfortunately, the typical response of most parents to a child's anger is to become angry in return. This is never helpful. Parents need to learn to strategically withdraw to gather together their own feelings. It is nearly impossible to teach self-control and discipline if one lacks it themselves. Often it is best for the child to experience the consequences of their own power. For example, if ones teenager becomes angry, looses control and punches a hole in the wall, it is a time for the parent to rejoice! Discipline becomes fairly easy, since they have cut their knuckles in the process. Of course, they have to patch the wall and paint it at their own expense. However, the parent does not have to beat them up as a form of discipline! There is a natural consequence to the child's out of control behavior. It will cost the child time and money, and they will suffer healthy shame and embarrassment when others see what they have done. To restate, the parent response is to strategically withdraw, ruthlessly avoiding a power struggle, while allowing natural and logical consequences to rain supreme. The parent must maintain control and act at a level of rationality above that of a child!

Unfortunately, many parents respond only slightly better than their child. Why take a child's statement or behavior personally? This is just a child! "My six year old said I was ugly and I fell apart. I'm hurt. How could they say that about me?" Get a life and grow up! A parent must develop a bit of a tough shell if they are going to have children and parent them properly. To love them beyond what they say or do can be a challenge, which becomes more difficult than necessary if the parent takes personally the words of the child, expressed in anger.

Along with avoiding a personal response, at the same time, build trust and respect by setting proper limits, and by showing unconditional love. The setting of limits, making clear what is acceptable and unacceptable in terms of the child's behavior, is an essential component to proper discipline and training. Thus, a parent who is unwilling to set limits will eventually have children who set unreasonable demands on the parents. This is never acceptable and always counter productive. The art of setting limits can be learned. Seeking the counsel of more experienced parents who have successfully set limits on their children could be most helpful.

Children are most complex and wonderful blessings. They seek power not to harm or hurt, but because the ability to have and manage power is an essential component of maturity. Children must learn to manage their own power in positive ways, finding appropriate expression over time. Thus, as a parent spends time with their child, coming to know them in all their uniqueness, they will naturally develop an appreciation for their abilities and expressions of power. These expressions will not be seen as rebellion, but an attempt to express the will of the child, both necessary and wanted. As with most any behavior, the parent must learn to manage the child, not squelch their will but mold it by the grace of God and patient parenting. Eventually, the child's expression of power will develop in the parent a sense of fascination and ultimately appreciation for the marvelous creation of God.

## Revenge

Once a parent has become aware of their own feelings of being hurt, a determination must be made as to the child's reason for taking revenge. What, if anything, did the parent do to cause harm or injury to the child? This can be a very difficult thing to determine, since often the parent may not have done anything at all. However, the child must believe that their parent has done something or they would not be acting out a theme of revenge[6]. Perhaps, it is someone else they are taking out their anger on,

---

[6] This is a generalization. There can be time when the child has learned that acting with revenge can get them what they want, as will using guilt for some parents. Thus, it is worth examining the possible reasons for the revenge, (continued on the next page)

yet the parent is the safe recipient of the child's anger. They also may be taking out their revenge for what someone else has done to them. This often happens when there is an abusive father or older sibling in the home. The children may take out their hurt on the mother. Often the child believes that the mom should protect them. If they perceive a lack of protection, since they cannot express anger at dad for fear of being severely punished, they will express it towards the "safer parent". When revenge is the goal of the child, the parent must resist responding in kind. Most parents fail miserably at this; all fail at times. Rather than acting in anger and punishment, a parent must:

1. Set a firm but loving boundary. Make a statement such as "That is unacceptable." "You're on time out!" or "Go to your room."
2. Look for the root of the anger. Often asking directly "What are you so angry at me about?" can bring a clear response. If not, the parent's role is to dispassionately state that the child's behavior will not be tolerated, since it is an inappropriate expression of anger or aggression.
3. Insure the child that, in spite of their vengeful actions, they are still loved, and always will be. Then repeat the request, give guidance, or respond according to the situation. Above all, resist the desire to utterly destroy the child!

## Inadequacy

Probably the most difficult child to deal with is the "inadequate" child. The best advice is to avoid criticism and do not give up on the child. Look for a strength that one can positively focus and build on. Understandably, this can be a hard search. However, once a strength is found, the parent will need to consistently reinforce their area of strength, even if it is something quite minor. Once found, continue to reinforce it, then look for other strengths. When they do not do things well or act with total "I can't" discouragement, avoid criticizing them and simply say, "I know you can. You *can* do it." Avoid rescuing them or doing everything for them. Eventually, the underlying cause will emerge.

---

but ultimately, the parent must still discipline and follow-through with the child, insuring compliance to rules clearly understood.

# An Example

We had a foster son named Ben. Ben had been abandoned twice. He was abandoned at two by his natural mother (due to severe medical problems, done in the best interest of Ben) and then the family that adopted him a few years later, unadopted him. He had significant emotional problems that his foster family was unable to deal with. He was a very difficult child who had had two obvious and devastating early life traumas.

Ben came to our home with an inability to trust and an internalized belief that rejection and abandonment would be his continual lot in life. He was always wondering, as demonstrated by his behavior but not his words, "Does anyone want me? Can I be loved, do I belong?" Whenever we decided as a family to go somewhere, we would inform Ben that we were going to be leaving at such and such a time, so Ben would be ready. He would never be ready! He would always ask, "Do you really want me to go?" It would frustrate all of us. "Of course, we want you to go." Finally, we would have to set a time limit. We will be leaving in ten minutes and if you are ready, be in the car, and we will go. If not, I guess you will stay here. In ten minutes, we left. The couple times we left him, he was devastated. However, rather than making a federal case out of the matter, we stated, "We told you ten minutes and you decided not to go. Next time be ready." Again, we did not beat him up over his decision or criticize him. We made him face the reality of his choice. Eventually (at least most of the time), Ben "pulled it together" in time to join the family. Unfortunately, he had a deep-rooted sense of inadequacy as a human being. The cause of this belief was fairly obvious, stemming from his tumultuous upbringing. Ben struggled with this problem continually, and no doubt does so to a greater or lessor degree to this day.

The whole purpose of understanding the goals of a child's behavior is to raise ones awareness of how to respond (versus react) when ones child triggers responses in the parent. If parents find themselves getting overly frustrated or increasingly angry, hurt, fearful, etc., becoming aware of it is the first step in effectively dealing with the feelings and the undesirable behavior in the child.

*"Consider it all joy by brethren when you encounter various trials."*

**James 1:2**

# Chapter 9

# Consequences

In figure (1) is presented a summary on logical consequences. When discussing discipline, depending upon the age of the child, logical consequences are an extremely effective method of correction. A logical consequence is different from a natural consequence. A natural consequence is; a child climbs a tree, you told him do not climb the tree, they fall out, they break their arm. The punishment is quite obvious, there is little need for additional intervention or an "I told you so" (though who can resist, really)! They have been punished; they do not need to be punished further. This is one form of a natural consequence. Another form would be when the child does not complete a chore which is required to receive playtime, they will not be able to play when they want to. However, in this form of natural consequence, a logical consequence to reinforce the natural one is highly effective. More on this later.

A logical consequence is one where the parent will actually consider the situation or the behavior of the child and develop a strategy for discipline, a punishment that fits the crime. That is basically all it is. It is logical in that it has something to do with or has a direct link with the behavior. If a child takes their parent's time in worry, etc. take their time. If they create a mess, give them an equal or greater mess to clean up. This tends to teach greater responsibility in the child and the consequences are only limited to a parents' imagination. Perhaps an example (an over exaggeration for illustration purposes) will help to clarify the meaning on this subject.

## Logical Consequences (Figure 1)

...an extremely effective method of correction

Although there are many methods of correction, one that is extremely effective is using logical consequences. This means planning a negative consequence that is logically related to the misbehavior.

Example: A child writes on the wall with a crayon. Logical consequence: the child cleans the wall.

Example: A child walks in and out of the house and forgets to close the door. What is the logical consequence?

The advantages of logical consequences:

1. It works!
2. It helps avoid a power struggle between the child and the parent.
3. It helps teach children responsibility.
4. It eliminates unnecessary nagging, corrections, and spankings.

Practice the planning of logical consequences. Jot down a logical consequence for each of the following situations...

Situation:

1. An eight-year-old child carelessly spills her milk.
2. John, age three, rides his tricycle into the busy street in front of his house.
3. A child makes his bed in the morning, but does is very sloppily. He has been taught how to make his bed and is capable of doing a neat job.
4. Danny, age six, walks through the kitchen tracking mud.
5. Amy, age nine, is consistently late for dinner.
6. Mark, age four, loves to play and will not come inside when he needs to go to the bathroom. He usually waits too long and then wets his pants on the way inside.
7. A nine-year-old continually leaves his skateboards, basketball, and toys all over the living room and family room.

8. Kelly, age ten, dresses slowly in the morning and doesn't care whether she is ready for school by her departure time of 7:30 or not.

## Mark and the Search for Cigarettes

Mark was another teenage foster child of ours. When he came to our home, as did many of the children we cared for, he had a smoking habit. We did not insist that he quit this nasty habit, but did set very clear boundaries on his smoking. For one, he could never smoke inside of the house or car, or in the front of our home. He would have to smoke in the backyard, where a "smoking zone" was set with a "butt" can for his residue. Unfortunately, Mark had an aversion, especially when his friends were with him, from placing the cigarette butts in the can. He loved to flick them all around the yard (the macho thing to do).

Not long after his arrival, and after a visit with some of his friends, we discovered butts around the yard. We make him pick them up and throw them away. No other consequence was given. Mercy reigned momentarily in our hearts. The second time this happened, he not only had to pick up his butts, but also he had a work job of tidying the backyard to near perfection. However, the lesson was still unlearned.

The third and final time Mark violated the rules, he encountered my wife and I in a different mood than before. We were less angry than amazed at the audacity of this insolent young whippersnapper! So we devised an insidious consequence.
We took a 5-gallon bucket, completely empty, and handed it to him. He asked, "What's this for?" We were delighted to inform Mark that he was on restriction forever, or at least until he filled this bucket to the rim with cigarette butts, but fill it he would. If we found other trash in the bucket when he was "through", he would have to start again. We smiled and left him with a widely gaping mouth and a look of bewilderment. What a gleeful sight it was.

It took Mark 7 days of searching through alleys, bars, friend's houses, etc., to fill the entire bucket. He reeked of cigarettes (our consequence) and complained through the whole event. When he was finished, I had the great enjoyment of dumping the can in the trashcan and requiring him to clean out the bucket. Nothing else was ever said, except to indicate to Mark that the 20-gallon can in the backyard would be the next can to fill. Needless to say, we never found another cigarette in our yard (from anyone, he policed it all!) during the rest of Mark's stay.

Another important point to remember is when a child is doing something inappropriate, an immediate response is not required. Most of the time, when disciplining a child, whether ones own or someone else's, a simple statement is effective, such as, "That is inappropriate, you owe me". In making this statement, the parent is essentially stating that they are the authority, and the child will be required to listen and respond accordingly. The normal response they give is "What?! What do I owe you?" At this point the parent can respond with confidence and in peace, "I'll tell you when I'm ready. Right now just go sit down." The sitting down and waiting for the parents' response is called, "time out", a powerful and highly effective tool in the parents' arsenal.

Time out requires that the child sit in a chair or in another designated place for a specified period of time. This can be in and of itself a very effective form of a logical consequence. The child is taking the parent's time and thus the parent takes the child's time. Time out is simply designed to give the child an opportunity to sit and think about what they have done. The time of time out is limited to about one minute for every year of life. A five-year-old should be able to tolerate five minutes of relative silence. If the parent attempts to make them sit in a chair longer than that, it will not work. What will ensue is an unnecessary and unproductive power struggle as the parent attempts to hold the child in their chair. This too often tried parental strategy is not logical; not effectual. Once the child is quietly sitting as per command and the time is waning, a wise parent will then ask of the child, "What did you do wrong?" Hopefully, the child will know what they have done to displease or violate clearly understood rules, and one can then make a logical correction. Ultimately, learning will occur as parents consistently apply positive discipline to the child.

As a child matures, a logical consequence always works best. If a child does not do their homework, what will the consequence be? Hopefully, the first consequence is they are going to receive a lower grade. That is a natural consequence of the child's irresponsible behavior. Of course, there is no such thing as double jeopardy in families! If they are being punished at school, they can also be punished at home! It is highly suggested that the parent link their school behavior to their home life as a part of purposeful parenting. This will reinforce the importance of school, and further reinforces the importance of being responsible.

To continue, one might also give them an additional consequence. For example, the parent might say, "You are obviously having a hard time managing your time, getting all your homework done in a timely manner. I guess you need to spend more time doing your homework, which means you need less time in front of the TV, listening to the stereo, talking on the phone with your friends, etc. So until we see you change this behavior, you must unplug the phone, put away your stereo speakers, etc." This would be a logical consequence; one that fits the crime.

Again, the primary focus is to teach responsible behavior, not to punish them. Remember one of the goals of all parents is to have an early retirement. It is difficult work being a hands on parent. My children have heard me say more than once that I am tired, and would love to retire as an overseeing parent. My hope was to become my children's friend, guide, anything but disciplinarian. Thus, my challenge to them was to fire me, by becoming responsible adults, able to take care of their own affairs without parental supervision. If they were taking care of their own business, they would not require outside parental intervention. In other words, as a family we could focus on having some fun together. However, as long as ones children are acting in such a way that they require being attended to, by all means, the parent must do so. That is the parents' responsibility. One must continue to parent, correct and control until they are of the age and maturity (age 18-21) to handle their own affairs, or until proven capable by their consistent behavior. Of course, the responsible behavior is generally progressive, and can be strong in one area (such as handling curfews) and weak in others (like doing homework). The goal is to encourage the child to progressively limit the need for parental involvement in terms of discipline and correction, by their progressively appropriate and responsible behavior.

Herewith is a last thought on natural and logical consequences. By all means, keep the consequences logical, not emotional. If the child takes time, take time. If the child takes or costs money, take money. On this later point, many parents have asked the question, "But what if they do not earn money?" The best strategy is to give them the opportunity to earn money that they do not get. How? By doing a work job that is a blessing to the family. In most cases, the parent will pay them and then charge them for their infraction. Thus, they actually have to feel the money in their hand and then watch it go away. It is a good lesson for them to learn. Much like learning to deal with the IRS!

## Some Other Methods

There are other methods of correction as well that are important and useful. Direct communication can be a highly effective way. A clear statement of the situation, the parental expectations and the consequences for disobedience is vital. Children need to know what is expected. If a child knows what is expected and they still do not do what is required, one has a clear reason to discipline them. Most parents (that is, those willing to look closely at the situation) find that the majority of problems at home are caused by a lack of communication. The children do not know what is expected of them. In fact, the rules and parental desires have not been adequately explained to them. When there are no written rules or expectations, what situations do arise can be interpreted in a number of ways. Both parents and children are gifted at interpreting rules to their own advantage. Most people prefer to do things with clear covenant agreements. Children need these as well. When available and clearly understood, it closes the door to misunderstanding, twisted interpretations, and significant confusion (Satan may be the author of confusion, but children and parents can appear as co-authors at times).

Another form of child discipline or teaching is reinforcement. Reinforcement means to strengthen a behavior by rewarding actions so they are more likely to be repeated in the future. Often this means catching someone doing something right. When a parent catches the child behaving in a commendable manner (yes, it is possible), a statement such as, "Wow, that was tremendous! You did a great job there." can increase the likelihood of it happening again. This positive and affirming statement will build them up and motivate them to repeat the positive behavior. But again, most parents will have to look for the positive. This is especially true with ones own children, or if a parent has been raised in a family system which expects good behavior as a duty, not needing affirming. Parents will often see the negative in their children, as it is easier to see.

In reality, all people tend to judge others according to their behavior, while judging oneself according to ones intention. Rarely do parents attempt to determine the intention of the child. What was the motivation of their heart? Most children want to please their parents, even into adulthood. They are not trying to disappoint or bring shame to the family. They were merely trying to do something right and they did it wrong. Often, children deserve some mercy. Remember, the Bible states that mercy triumphs over judgment. As one shows mercy, so one will receive mercy.

Sometimes physical spanking, applied appropriately, and with the right attitude, can bring change. Now, what is the right attitude? The proper attitude is always love, bringing discipline designed for the correction of the child. At what age is spanking no longer an effective method of discipline? It seems as though mild spanking is only effective to age seven or eight. Beyond that, it only makes the parent feel better to hit their child. It does nothing to or for the child. Parents may feel better, having had opportunity to vent their understandable frustration.

I was presenting a workshop on Parenting on Purpose in Alabama. When I came to the topic of child discipline, a man of about 50 spoke up. The conference was for a group of singles and single parents. The man said he had a twenty-seven year old daughter, who came home for a visit at Christmas time. He stated that they had a heated conversation, and when she disagreed with his politics he slapped her "head around." I asked him, "How was jail?" "What do you mean jail? That girl better never lip off to me." Half the room said, "Right on brother." A twenty-seven year old daughter! In truth, that is assault! People generally go to jail for such behavior. Many in the room thoroughly believed that his action was acceptable and appropriate. How utterly ludicrous! "That daughter respects me," he stated. She may fear him, but she most likely harbors deep resentment and could very likely be a candidate for domestic violence when and if she were to marry. Further, when and if she had children, child abuse could be a concern, with herself as the perpetrator or her husband, since she would most likely lack the psychological means to protect her children from similar assault. How tragic.

The motivation of the heart of a responsible parent (especially a Christian one) is to correct, not to hurt. Thus, as much as it lies within the power of the parent, one must make sure not to discipline/punish out of anger. Most adults have failed in that regard at one time or another. One should not lament but repent. Learning from past mistakes and poor parenting models from the past will assist the parent to take responsibility and grow. This is truly all the Lord expects from any of His children. With His help and the loving guidance of experienced leaders in the Body of Christ, it is possible and probable to grow.

Along with the principles of discipline listed above, provided here are some helpful suggestions that parents can put into practice to strengthen their parenting skills.

1. **Firmness.** Showing firmness or fairness in judgment, friendliness in attitude, concise with a conviction of feeling helps children know where they stand. A parent can be firm and do so fairly versus showing strictness which is just demanding rigorous conformity. There is a difference between the two and parenting on purpose fights to find that fine line.

2. **Setting limits**. This is a prescribed boundary, a set of rules that are flexible, but clear. Depending upon the age of the child, the limits should not be overly permissive. When children have no rules and are allowed to do whatever they feel, children will experience a lack of security, often leading to acting out behavior. All nature abhors a vacuum, and when the parent will not parent, the child will!

3. **Expressing caution**. Friendly warnings to avoid damage or suffering versus voicing threats. Every parent, at one time or another has tried to threaten their child. How long does it work? As long as they are within ear shot. As soon as the parent is out of sight, the threat no longer works. If a threat is to be given, or a promise made, be willing to follow it up. But think about the threat or promise before it is made. Many a parent has made a rash statement such as, "You are going to be on restriction for the next five years, or until Jesus returns!" Of course, the parent will just have to eat those words. There is no way a parent in their right mind (it is true what they say, insanity is inherited, you get it from your children) is going to supervise a child's restriction for five years.

4. **Being consistent**. Consistency helps to build security. When the parent provides consistent love, support, follow through, guidance and meaningful communication they effectively create an environment for growth. No parent is perfectly consistent, but this should remain as a personal goal.

5. **Using Comparisons**. Comparisons are generally unfair and quite counter-productive. The only comparison that is useful is comparing the child's actual behavior from an agreed upon and semi-objective standard. Resist at all costs comparing ones child with another sibling, cousin, friend or self. This only causes resentment and discouragement.

6. **Upgrading**. Statements of praise versus downgrading, belittling criticism, etc. It has been said that sticks and stones can break our bones, but words…they can destroy. When a parent makes unkind statements to their child, they can be forgiven but never voided. Thus, great care must be taken in the words used. Also, children will quickly pick-up the

negative and degrading statements made to a spouse, and attitudes of disrespect for the same of opposite sex can be passed on by unkind and harmful words.

7. **Expressing feelings**. Permitting ones child to express versus suppress their feelings appropriately is healthy. If a child is angry with a parent, they have a right to speak, but they need to learn to do so respectfully. This actually teaches skills for adult living, skills that are vitally needed in the real world. As with most things, children will not be highly appropriate and articulate the first few times they express anger or other strong emotions, yet they should be encouraged, and corrected with grace and mercy.

## Building an Image of Health

Parenting on purpose, and ultimately all of the effort made to parent children, is designed to build a Godly self-concept, with the characteristics of self confidence, inner security and the ability to control emotions. Without positive parenting the opposite may occur, self-confidence can be destroyed, inner security violated, and the ability to control emotions removed, leading to an image of rejection versus acceptance. All parents want to see their children feel accepted, worthwhile and successful. Parents have a wonderful opportunity to assist in the process of making and molding children into adults that will be pleasing to the Lord.

There are some simple things that can be done as a family to strengthen a healthy, Godly self-concept:

1. **Develop family tasks**. In every household, there are many tasks to complete. I have jokingly said that one of the reasons my wife and I had children was to have someone to do the work around the house. This is not the case, but having children necessitates teaching them to be workers not just consumers. Thus, it is important to create a list of household tasks. When parents take the time to do this, they generally find that there are a lot of them. One of the greatest conflicts in marriages has to do with who is going to do what. Usually the mom feels as though she is doing everything and in many cases she is.

Listing the tasks and assigning a child to be held responsible for them can minimize family stress, while teaching vital skills. Each child needs chores to do at their level of developmental capability. A family meeting can be very productive in terms of structuring the family or putting ones house in order. In the meeting, the family can develop a daily work/planning chart that lists the day of the week and who are to do what chore. With the list, each member of the family (yes, even dad) is held accountable for accomplishing what they are responsible for. It is a tool for learning and united team building.

## Keep in Mind the Goal

The majority of Christians want to develop family systems that are going to be positive and healthy. In order to discipline, to train, one must separate past learned models from ones present family, and without making unnecessary and unfair comparisons with other families. All children are unique and all families will reflect that uniqueness. Ones goal is to encourage independence. Parents need to stop trying to be good. There is only one who is good. He is God. The rest of the world falls woefully short. Parents need to stay focused on their own responsibilities. Part of doing this is to not focus on others. Do not compare your family with other families. The dynamics that make up another home may be far removed from ones own family

**A parents' goal is to be one step healthier than ones family of origin.** For many, that is not too difficult a task. The fact one is not beating their children half to death is probably a sign of progress, demonstrating that the parent is doing a good job compared to past experience. However, do not settle for mediocrity. God calls His children to be the best possible, as He provides grace and strength, and as one applies the word of truth judiciously. Much of this will come with a willingness to talk less and act more. Parents need to talk much less, and act more, with consistency and righteousness. Children respond to what they see their parents do. More often than not, fathers understand this better than mothers do. A father can lift an eyebrow and give a clear and profound message, "Move again and you are dead!" It is nothing personal. As Bill Cosby says, "I brought you in, I'll take you out." Moms tend to use their verbal skills most. Stop, stop, stop, stop, stop, stop! When they finally get to a predetermined decibel level, that is when the children learn that they must respond or mom's going to start hitting! If parents talk less and act more, this will initially disrupt the equilibrium of the children's minds. The point is it is through ones loving action, consistent follow through, positive example, effective energy on behalf of ones children, which are in many ways a parent's best investment. As with any investment, when a parent finds good soil, as in the tender hearts and minds of children, and the good seed of love, discipline, education, spiritual guidance, God's Word, etc., is sown or invested in their hearts, the seed will produce a rich harvest. What will be produced will be a loving, responsible adult that a parent will have glowing pride in. May God help every parent to be such an investor as they *Parent on Purpose*.

*"Faith is the substance of things hoped for, the evidence of things not seen."*

**Hebrews 11:1**

# Chapter 10

## A Final Look At God's Word

There is much to be applied from the writings of James to parenting. Though his writing can appear hard, it is filled with wisdom for Parenting on Purpose.

In James 1:2 it says, *"Consider it all joy my brethren when you encounter various trials."* Parenting can be the biggest trial one will ever face. Most parents feel tried, convicted and sentenced to many, many years of hard labor. It does not have to be. Hindsight does give one certain perspective. Remember that, "Knowing that the testing of your faith, produces endurance." Endurance is certainly needed to parent effectively, as well as having a visionary view to the future.

Most parents need a greater sense of their own importance, and need to recognize how desperately their children need them. It is good for parents to acknowledge the fact that they are needed by their children for the long haul. Parents continue the process of being influential with their children their whole lives, just as ones own parents are still somewhat influential. In light of this truth, one does not need instantaneous wisdom for every situation. But parents do need endurance.

In most families, children bring out the worst in their parents. Do not fear this fact but embrace in a positive way the truth by recognizing ones own fallibility. No parent is perfect; no human is able to judge. The primary need is to recognize the areas where growth is needed, and submit these areas to God's word and wise counsel. Again, admit when angry, frustrated, or when the desire to "ring their little necks" emerges. It is neither wise nor judicious to express these feelings to the children, but certainly to the Lord and maybe to someone else so that continued growth in grace and accountability can occur.

James continues, *"And let endurance have its perfect result that you may be perfect and complete lacking nothing."* Through endurance a parent can become perfect. That word perfect means equipped, fully prepared or ready for the task at hand. Most parents have felt woefully inadequate for the task of parenting, do to lack of training and experience. It is through the enduring, with the help of the Holy Spirit, that one can become equipped for greater service. Past experiences can be utilized for good, as they are related to daily life, recognizing that God has helped thus far and He will continue to help for the future.

> Verse five says, *"But if any of you lacks wisdom, let him ask of God who gives to all men generously and without reproach. And it will be given to him. But let him ask in faith, without any doubting. For the one who doubts is like the surf of the sea, driven and tossed by the wind. For let not that man expect that he will receive anything from the Lord, being a double minded man, unstable in all his ways."*

Parents must be united, having a common set of beliefs and values that will be portrayed in front of the children and communicated to them with clarity. It is certainly true that God expects parents to act in wisdom. Wisdom literally means to allow the Word of God to be pounded down into one's head until it becomes incorporated into one's life. The process of having the word do its work in equipping and maturing the life of a believer is arduous, and often appears a remote possibility. However, the scripture indicates that wisdom may be obtained by anyone who will ask the Lord for it.

It also says later in the book of James, *"you have not because you ask not or you ask amiss in order to consume it upon your own lusts."* (James 4:3) Most readers tend to sexualize or sensualize this statement. It has a much broader meaning. In context, it has to do with using something for one's own selfish gain, regardless of the item being used. Most parents desire to learn parenting techniques so that they can win the power struggle between themselves and their children. The only way one can truly win is if everyone does. Families are supposed to be win/win organizations.

Thus, a parent must be willing to ask for wisdom from the Lord who will freely give it. Be assured, God will pound wisdom into the mind of any willing parent. He will take His word and pound it in until a full, adequate and applicable understanding is obtained. Assuredly, one must believe that He will do it. Faith is necessary for any part of our spiritual or natural journey. *"Faith is the substance of things hoped for, the evidence of things not seen."* (Hebrews 11:1). For certain, a parent may not see the wisdom of God quickly, but a parent asks the Lord hears, and is already providing it.

## A Final Thought

Whether you are a single parent or a united family, your situation may seem hopeless, but it is not serious. God is with you. If He is for you, who can stand against you? Who stands in the place of opposition against the Lord God? However, do not be foolish. Do not think that you have all the answers if you do not. Be honest with yourself. Keep asking questions. Be willing to read, be willing to study, because it is not just for you that you are parenting. Remember you are called of God to prepare the next generation, a generation who will be pure, untarnished by the defilement experienced in the generation of the 60's, 70's and 80's. Our greatest hope for the world is the generation now being parented. If they are properly trained, they will be able to take the gospel of Jesus to the world and change the world as we know it. This task, though awesome, should not be a burden; it should be a joy. Knowing that God has a plan and purpose for your parenting makes the effort worth enduring. Through parenting on purpose, the purpose being to bring children to maturity and prepare them for leadership is to fulfill ones destiny in God.

# APPENDICES

# APPENDIX I

# TIPS FOR PARENTS

## WAYS OF GIVING ACCEPTABLE GUIDANCE:

1. **Be sure that the child understands**. Have his attention when you speak. Use understandable words. Give one direction at a time. Show him as well as tell him.

2. **Give advance warning when asking child to change from one activity to another**. Don't expect him to stop instantly; let him finish his activity if at all practical. Small children become confused when hurried. Forcing a child to perform too quickly or to turn abruptly from one activity to another often causes frustration, irritation and conflict.

3. **Be matter-of-fact**. Take compliance for granted. The attitude should be, "We all do this." If he says, "No", don't take it so seriously that you argue the point or become excited. Most often he will comply if the adult remains calm, as he is usually just "testing".

4. **Limit directions to essentials**. Release the child from constant heckling. Over-direction breeds rebellion.

5. **Be quiet in manner and tone**. Don't take his non-compliance as an affront to your dignity as an adult.

6. **Suggest the next specific act when a child dawdles**. "Where is your towel?" When a child continues handwashing too long, or just offer him a towel. "What did you do with your napkin?" When he gets stuck in finishing his food. Such comments recall to him his task, but leave the initiative with him.

7. **Rejoice with the child** when he achieves something important to him, no matter how small. Tell him what you like about what he does. The more problems a child has, the more he needs successes and favorable recognition.

8. **Give the child a choice of action when feasible**. "Where would you like to park your trike, here or over there?" gives him personal interest in the situation and develops his initiative and independence.

9. **Give the child a choice only when you can accept a negative reply**. (Never give the child a choice however when his safety is involved or when it is interfering with others.) Don't ask "Would you like to take

a nap now" when the subject isn't open for refusal. The child should only be offered when a "No" can be accepted.

10. **<u>Help the child only when he needs help</u>**. Don't impose your ideas upon him, but encourage him to find out for himself. This builds independence and imagination.

Source Unknown

# APPENDIX II – CHILD'S MISTAKEN GOALS

| Goals of Misbehavior | What a child is saying | How Parent Feels | Child's Reaction to Reprimand | Some Corrective Measures |
|---|---|---|---|---|
| ATTENTION | I only count when I am being noticed or served. | Annoyed. Wants to remind, coax. Delighted with "good" child | Temporarily stops disturbing action when given attention. | Ignore. Answer or do the unexpected. Give attention at pleasant times. |
| POWER | I only count when I am dominating, when you do what I want you to do. | Provoked. Generally wants power. Challenged "I'll make him do it." "You can't get away with it.' | Wants to get even. Makes self disliked. | Extricate self. Act, not talk. Be friendly. Encouragement. Establish equality. Redirect child's efforts into constructive channels. |
| REVENGE | I can't be liked, I don't have power, but I'll count if I can hurt others as I feel hurt by life. | Hurt, mad. "How could he do this to me." | Wants to get even. Makes self disliked. | Extricate self. Win child. Maintain order with minimum restraint. Avoid retaliations. Take time and effort to help child. |
| INADEQUACY | I can't do anything right so I won't try to do anything at all; I am no good. | Despair "I give up" | No reprimand, therefore, no reaction. Feels there is no use to try. Passive. | Encouragement (may take long). Faith in child ability. |

# APPENDIX III – CHOOSING A METHOD OF CORRECTION

| METHOD | DEFINITION | EXAMPLES | WHEN USED |
|---|---|---|---|
| **COMMUNICATION** | A clear statement of the situation, your expectations, and the consequences for disobedience. Ask the child to repeat what you have said to make sure you were heard. Invite questions of understanding or comments as appropriate. | | |
| **NATURAL CONSEQUENCES** | Staying out of the way letting nature run its course. (Some natural consequences, of course, are too dangerous or serious-like failing a course in school) to allow a child to experience it if other measures could prevent. | | |
| **LOGICAL CONSEQUENCES** | Planning a negative consequence that is logically related to this misbehavior. | | |

# APPENDIX III – CHOOSING A METHOD OF CORRECTION

| METHOD | DEFINITION | EXAMPLES | WHEN USED |
|---|---|---|---|
| **REINFORCEMENT** | Strengthening or rewarding actions so that they are more likely to be repeated in the future. | | |
| **EXTINCTION** | Not rewarding a negative behavior with attention so that it will be eliminated. | | |
| **PHYSICAL SPANKING** | Physical pain, applied appropriately and with the right attitude. | | |

# APPENDIX IV - DAILY WORK PLANNER CHART

| DAY OF THE WEEK | MOM | DAD | #1 CHILD | #2 CHILD | #3 CHILD | #4 CHILD | #5 CHILD |
|---|---|---|---|---|---|---|---|
| SUNDAY | | | | | | | |
| MONDAY | | | | | | | |
| TUESDAY | | | | | | | |
| WEDNESDAY | | | | | | | |
| THURSDAY | | | | | | | |
| FRIDAY | | | | | | | |
| SATURDAY | | | | | | | |

## APPENDIX V - WEEKLY CALENDAR

| DAY OF WEEK | SUN. | MON. | TUES. | WED. | THURS. | FRI. | SAT. |
|---|---|---|---|---|---|---|---|
| MORNING | | | | | | | |
| NOON | | | | | | | |
| NIGHT | | | | | | | |

# APPENDIX VI

| | PRACTICE |
|---|---|
| **Showing FIRMNESS** | Fairness in judgment. Friendliness in attitude. Conciseness in requests. Conviction in feeling. |
| **Setting LIMITS** | Prescribe boundaries. Set rules that are flexible. Define standards. |
| **Expressing CAUTION** | Friendly warnings to avoid personal damage or suffering. |
| **Showing CONSEQUENCES** | Permitting suffering resulting from the child's actions related to the situation. |
| **Being CONSISTENT** | Continuous agreement with oneself. Compatible attitudes with other parent in front of child. |
| **Using COMPARISON** | Showing only the differences and similarities of the child in regard to his own behavior. |
| **UP-GRADING** | Statements (praise) designed to build up the child's feelings of his own worth and adequacy |
| **Expressing FEELINGS** | Permitting the child to express and release hostile and angry feelings. Accepting the child's feelings but not permitting anti-social behavior. |
| These measures BUILD self-confidence, inner-security, and ability to control emotions. They give the child a feeling of **ACCEPTANCE**. ||

# APPENDIX VI

| | AVOID |
|---|---|
| Showing **STRICTNESS** | Demanding rigorous conformity. Harshness in actions. Unfriendliness in feeling. Unyielding in attitude. |
| Being **OVERLY-PERMISSIVE** | Laxity in regard to, or absence of, definite rules, regulations, and standards for the child. |
| Voicing **THREATS** | Expression of actions designed to inflict injury or damage to the child's ego and personal welfare. |
| Planning **PUNISHMENT** | Deliberate and planned suffering to the child's ego through fear, by means of bodily hurts, denial of privileges, or isolation. |
| Being **INCONSISTENT** | Contradicting oneself in relation to previously stated attitudes. Contradicting the other parent in front of the child. |
| Using **COMPARISON** | Voicing unfavorable differences and similarities with brothers, sisters, or other children. |
| **DOWN-GRADING** | Statements (belittling, fault-finding) designed to lower the status and self-esteem of the child in his own eyes. |
| Suppressing **FEELINGS** | Causing the child to feel guilty and inwardly upset by making him keep his hostile and angry feelings within him. |
| | These measures **DESTROY** self-confidence, inner security and ability to control emotions. They give the child a feeling of **REJECTION**. |

# APPENDIX VII

# A Memorandum From your Child

Adapted from
*"The King's Business Magazine"*

1. Don't spoil me. I know quite well that I ought not to have all I ask for. I'm only testing you.

2. Don't be afraid to be firm with me. I prefer it. It lets me know where I stand.

3. Don't be inconsistent. That confuses me and makes me try harder to get away with everything I can.

4. Don't make promises. You might not be able to keep them. That will discourage my trust in you.

5. Don't fall for my provocations when I say and do things just to upset you. Then I'll try for more victories.

6. Don't do things for me that I can do for myself. It makes me feel like a baby, and I will continue to put you in my service.

7. Don't let my bad habits get me a lot of attention. It only encourages me to continue them.

8. Don't correct me in front of people. I'll take much more notice if you talk quietly to me in private.

9. Don't try to discuss my behavior in the heat of a conflict. For some reason my hearing is not very good at this time and my cooperation is even worse. It is all right to take the action required, but let's not talk about it until later.

10. Don't make me feel that all of my mistakes are sins. I have to learn to make mistakes without feeling that I am no good. I don't have to be perfect to be somebody.

# BIBLIOGRAPHY

1. Andolfi, Maurizio. *Family Therapy – An Interactional Approach.* Plenum Press, New York and London.

2. Bohac, Joseph. *Human Development.* Vision Publishing, Ramona, CA.

3. Chant, Ken. *Pentecostal Pulpit.* Vision Publishing, Ramona, CA.

4. Chant, Ken. *Understanding The Bible.* Vision Publishing, Ramona, CA.

5. Corfman, Eunice. *Families Today.* U.S. Department of Health, Education, and Welfare.

6. DeKoven, Stan. *Marriage and Family Life.* Vision Publishing, Ramona, CA.

7. Dinkmeyer, Donold. *Systematic Training for Effective Parenting.*

8. Dobson, James. *Dare To Discipline.* Tyndale House, Carol Stream, IL.

9. Dreikurs, Rudolf. *Children the Challenge.* Penguin Group, New York, NY.

10. Framo, Ph.D., James L. *Explorations in Marital and Family Therapy.* Springer Publishing Company, New York.

11. Haley, Jay and Hoffman, Lynn. *Techniques of Family Therapy.* Basic Books, Inc., New York.

12. Hauser, Stuart T. *Adolescents and Their Families.* The Free Press, New York.

13. Rhodes, Sonya and Wilson, Josleen. *Surviving Family Life.* G.P. Putnam's Sons, New York.

14. Rice, John R., *The Home: Courtship, Marriage and Children.* Zondervan Publishing House, Grand Rapids, MI.

15. Swindoll, Charles R. *Growing Wise in Family Life.* Multinomah Press, Portland, OR.

16. Turner, Ralph H., *Family Interaction.* John Wiley & Sons, Inc., New York.

17. Wright, H. Norman. *Marital Counseling: A Biblically Based Behavioral, Cognitive Approach.* Christian Marriage Enrichment, Denver, CO.

www.ingramcontent.com/pod-product-compliance
Lightning Source LLC
Chambersburg PA
CBHW032001080426
42735CB00007B/474